Open Minds, Devoted Hearts

HORIZONS *in* RELIGIOUS EDUCATION is a book series sponsored by the Religious Education Association: An Association of Professors, Practitioners and Researchers in Religious Education. It was established to promote new scholarship and exploration in the academic field of Religious Education. The series will include both seasoned educators and newer scholars and practitioners just establishing their academic writing careers.

Books in this series reflect religious and cultural diversity, educational practice, living faith, and the common good of all people. They are chosen on the basis of their contributions to the vitality of religious education around the globe. Writers in this series hold deep commitments to their own faith traditions, yet their work sets forth claims that might also serve other religious communities, strengthen academic insight, and connect the pedagogies of religious education to the best scholarship of numerous cognate fields.

The posture of the Religious Education Association has always been ecumenical and multi-religious, attuned to global contexts, and committed to affecting public life. These values are grounded in the very institutions, congregations, and communities that transmit religious faith. The association draws upon the interdisciplinary richness of religious education connecting theological, spiritual, religious, social science and cultural research and wisdom. Horizons of Religious Education aims to heighten understanding and appreciation of the depth of scholarship resident within the discipline of religious education, as well as the ways it impacts our common life on a fragile world. Without a doubt, we are inspired by the wonder of teaching and the awe that must be taught.

Jack L. Seymour (chair), Garrett-Evangelical Theological Seminary

Dean G. Blevins, Nazarene Theological Seminary

Dori Grinenko Baker, The Fund for Theological Education & Sweet Briar College

Randy Litchfield, Methodist Theological School in Ohio

Sondra H. Matthaei, Saint Paul School of Theology

Siebren Miedema, Vrije Universiteit Amsterdam

Hosffman Ospino, Boston College

Mai-Anh Le Tran, Eden Theological Seminary

Anne Streaty Wimberly, Interdenominational Theological Seminary

Open Minds, Devoted Hearts

Portraits of Adult Religious Educators

SARAH M. TAUBER

◌PICKWICK *Publications* · Eugene, Oregon

OPEN MINDS, DEVOTED HEARTS
Portraits of Adult Religious Educators

Horizons in Religious Education 2

Copyright © 2015 Sarah M. Tauber. All rights reserved. Except for brief quotations in critical publications or reviews, no part of this book may be reproduced in any manner without prior written permission from the publisher. Write: Permissions, Wipf and Stock Publishers, 199 W. 8th Ave., Suite 3, Eugene, OR 97401.

Pickwick Publications
An Imprint of Wipf and Stock Publishers
199 W. 8th Ave., Suite 3
Eugene, OR 97401

www.wipfandstock.com

ISBN 13: 978-1-4982-1876-4

Cataloging-in-Publication data:

Tauber, Sarah M.

Open minds, devoted hearts : portraits of adult religious educators / Sarah M. Tauber.

xvi + 168 p. ; 23 cm. —Includes bibliographical references.

Horizons in Religious Education 2

ISBN 13: 978-1-4982-1876-4

1. Jewish religious education of adults. I. Series. II. Title.

DS113 T35 2015

Manufactured in the USA

Table of Orientations to teaching Bible from *Textual Knowledge: Teaching the Bible in Theory and Practice* (New York: JTS 2003). Reprinted by permission of the publisher, JTS, and author, Barry W. Holtz.

For my parents Joseph and Phyllis, and for my children Benjamin and Hannah, with abundant gratitude and abiding love

CONTENTS

Series Foreword ix
Preface xi
Acknowledgments xv

Introduction 1
    Chapter 1   Foundational Theories and New Advances 17
    Chapter 2   The Gardener 39
    Chapter 3   The Midwife 62
    Chapter 4   The Learner 83
    Chapter 5   Rabbis as Facilitators 102
    Chapter 6   Rabbis as Co-Learners 118
    Chapter 7   Rabbis as Community Builders 133
    Chapter 8   A Clergy for Our Time 149

Appendix A   Consent Letter 159
Appendix B   Open Ended Semi-Structured Interview Questions 161

Bibliography 163

SERIES FOREWORD

HORIZONS in RELIGIOUS EDUCATION defines a book series sponsored by the Religious Education Association: An Association of Professors, Practitioners and Researchers in Religious Education. The REA founded this series to promote new scholarship and exploration in the academic field of Religious Education. The series includes both seasoned educators alongside newer scholars and practitioners just establishing their academic writing careers.

Books in this series reflect religious and cultural diversity, educational practice, living faith, and the common good of all people. They are chosen on the basis of their contributions to the vitality of religious education around the globe. Writers in this series hold deep commitments to their own faith traditions, yet their work sets forth claims that might also serve other religious communities, strengthen academic insight, and connect the pedagogies of religious education to the best scholarship of numerous cognate fields.

The posture of the Religious Education Association has always been ecumenical and multi-religious, attuned to global contexts, and committed to affecting public life. The REA establishes these values in the very institutions, congregations, and communities that transmit religious faith. The association draws upon the interdisciplinary richness of religious education connecting theological, spiritual, religious, social science, and cultural research and wisdom. *HORIZONS in RELIGIOUS EDUCATION* aims to heighten understanding and appreciation of the depth of scholarship resident within the discipline of religious education, as well as the ways it impacts our common life on a fragile world. Without a doubt, we are inspired by the wonder of teaching and the awe that must be taught.

—Dean Blevins, former president of REA and Professor of Practical Theology and Christian Discipleship at Nazarene Theological Seminary in Kansas City, MO, USA Co-chair, Horizons Editorial Board

PREFACE

Religious faith is to be lived. Religious faith affects our relationships with the deepest and richest mysteries of our living and our world. Religious faith profoundly affects our commitments—how we engage others in our communities and beyond; what we hold precious and dear; for what we are willing to work and sacrifice; to what we give our material and spiritual resources; and what world we seek to build and with whom.

While many people continue to grow and deepen religious commitments, we know that others stagnate or retreat in fear. Why? How can we help people thrive in faith commitments and seek to affect the world that surrounds them? We, religious educators, are convinced that a faith tradition needs to be taught and its multiple means of expression need to be explored. Rarely are religious communities univocal. While holding to a common set of practices, beliefs, ritual expressions, or values, each religious community embodies a range of diverse expressions as they are affected by culture, context, and public events. How a person of faith negotiates the terrain of living and contributes to the wider health and thriving of it is an essential question and task of religious education.

The editorial board of the *REA—HORIZONS in RELIGIOUS EDUCATION* is delighted to add Sarah Tauber's manuscript as the second in our series. It provides a glimpse into how three religious leaders seek to guide their adult participants so that they will grow in faith. In fact, more specifically, these rabbis nurture, help birth, and are co-learners in the process of faithfulness. Writing from her Jewish tradition, a tradition that has always honored learning and demonstrates over and over how to connect knowing, doing and being, Dr. Tauber reclaims the crucial and ongoing task of adult education. While immersed in the vitality of a tradition, the insights of this book speak from this tradition to others. It will promote a lively conversation among persons of different religious communities. One from

Preface

which we all will learn and benefit. She offers models and directions to enhance the wider practices of religious educators and of clergy education. The book fulfills the hope of REA that religious communities learn from each other and together contribute to the shaping of the common good.

As the title reflects, Dr. Tauber demonstrates how education helps people deepen devotion to a path—drawing on ancient resources in a living world. Furthermore, she helps us see how learning is also an open and engaged process where the people of faith contribute to the ongoing shaping and developing of those religious traditions. What are the tasks and roles educators, clergy, and religious leaders draw on in fulfilling their vocations? In fact, how do they understand the vocation of teaching and learning itself? We thank her for this textured richness.

Texture—yes, that is a fine word to define this book. Dr. Tauber demonstrates how scholarship and practice are intimately connected. She uses a rich qualitative method of research —portraiture—where we enter deeply and profoundly into another's expression of her or his vocation. The method provides a rich and nuanced "portrait"/ model for us. Of course, each portrait inspires us with understandings and practices. Yet, each portrait teaches us that we too are responsible for embodying our vocation of living and teaching the faith.

We suggest you breathe in the fragrance of each portrait, pay attention to the ways you live out your faith, attend to your religious convictions, and enhance your work and leadership. Indeed may the book enable those in your community to enhance your open minds and devoted hearts.

—Jack L. Seymour, Professor of Religious Education at Garrett-Evangelical Theological Seminary, Evanston, Illinois, USA Co-chair, Horizons Editorial Board

—Elizabeth Caldwell, Harold Blake Walker Professor Emerita of Pastoral Theology of McCormick Theological Seminary in Chicago, Illinois, USA Co-chair, Horizons Editorial Board

HORIZONS IN RELIGIOUS EDUCATION—EDITORIAL REVIEW BOARD

Jack L. Seymour, Garrett-Evangelical Theological Seminary, Evanston, IL, USA Co-chair

Dean G. Blevins, Nazarene Theological Seminary, Kansas City, MO, USA Co-chair

Elizabeth Caldwell, McCormick Theological Seminary, Chicago, IL, USA Co-chair

Dori Grinenko Baker, The Fund for Theological Education and Sweet Briar College, Sweet Briar, VA, USA

Sondra H. Matthaei, Saint Paul School of Theology, Leawood, KS, USA

Siebren Miedema, Vrije Universiteit, Amsterdam, The Netherlands

Hosffman Ospino, Boston College, Chestnut Hill, MA, USA

Mai-Anh Le Tran, Eden Theological Seminary, Webster Groves, MO, USA

Anne Streaty Wimberly, Interdenominational Theological Seminary, Atlanta, GA, USA

ACKNOWLEDGMENTS

Throughout the journey that culminated in this book, I have been blessed by the guidance, support, and wisdom of many individuals. My gratitude to them is everlasting.

The three rabbis portrayed here set aside many hours from their very busy schedules to participate in the extensive interviews with me. Their willingness to include me in their classes, welcome me into their congregations, and continue the conversation once the formal process was completed allowed the project to blossom beyond my expectations. My appreciation goes also to the adult learners in their respective synagogues. They graciously shared their honest and insightful reflections about Jewish learning and rabbis as teachers, and in so doing enriched my research. Carol Ingall, my dissertation adviser, provided me with the steadfast encouragement of an outstanding mentor and scholar through the years. Mary Boys, Barry Holtz, Jeff Kress, and Jack Wertheimer have provided helpful criticism along the way. The editors of the *Journal of Jewish Education* published portions of my research as articles that enabled me to refine my thinking about the subject. Phoebe Atkinson and Ana Ibanez gave me the drive necessary to complete the project. Donald Billingsley and Ismar Schorsch each independently persuaded me to forge on and turn my dissertation research into a book.

My deepest gratitude to the Religious Education Association (REA) for choosing this work as the second in the Horizon Series. In particular, Jack Seymour was a font of guidance. Raquel da Rosa, editor and interlocutor par excellence, was the perfect partner for bringing the manuscript to its final form. The many educators and adult learners whom I have taught and learned from over the years, including my students at the Jewish Theological Seminary, motivate me in my work as a teacher and a scholar. Their

Acknowledgments

passion for and commitment to learning gives me hope for the promising future of adult religious education.

Jewish tradition embraces the bonds that connect the generations. The unstinting support of my parents and children throughout the years that this project has continued is without a doubt why it has reached fruition. The wisdom of my parents and the spiritedness of my children are qualities that inspire me in my work every day. I dedicate this book to them.

INTRODUCTION

Our youngest was two or two and a half and my husband was giving her a bath and out of the blue she turned to Jacob and she said, "Abba, God loves boys better than girls." Had it been me, I certainly would have said, "Oh, no, that's no true." But Jacob was a much wiser parent. He said, "What makes you say that?" And she said, "Well, God has a penis and boys have a penis so God likes boys better." Now, I learned two things from this . . . which were that the pronoun is not neutral, and until then we said it was—you know, "It's not really He . . . we don't really know." But she got it, that it does matter. The other is that the way we see ourselves through our religious lens has a huge impact on how we value ourselves. And because she saw herself as worth less in God's eyes, in some cosmic way, she was worth less. So religion is really powerful, and finding ways to connect certainly with adult learners how religion has impacted them and how it continues to, and how it has the power to shape who we are and who we are in the world, is at the core of sacred learning . . . So I really do believe that what we say creates universes, and particularly what we say in the name of our religious traditions.
—Rabbi Rina Lewin[1]

Say the word "rabbi" to someone and it inevitably evokes a multitude of images and emotions. Rarely are they neutral. For two millennia rabbis have been fixtures on the landscape of Western civilization. Whether praised as scholars and Jewish communal leaders or designated as the religious representatives of a persecuted minority, rabbis often have been viewed from within and without as the symbolic exemplars of Judaism. From Rabbi Akiba in the talmudic era, to Maimonides in the medieval period, to Abraham Joshua Heschel in the twentieth century, Jews and others have looked

---

1. All names are pseudonyms to protect the identity of the rabbis.

to rabbis for leadership, wisdom, insight, and uplift. Nothing less than the survival of Judaism itself is the charge delivered to the doorstep of every rabbi. And, for much of history, and in many far-flung realms, rabbis have made good on these demands. What, then, of today's American rabbi?

Over the past two decades I have been a member of four synagogues, two in the United States and two in Europe. In each I have participated in adult learning as a student and as a Jewish educator. In one I taught adults in my capacity as a professional employed by the congregation as its education director. Over the years, and in particular during the time that I regularly taught adults, I began asking questions about the purposes of adult learning, especially adult religious education; about the nature of the relationship between the teachers and their adult learners; and about the differences between teaching adults and teaching children and adolescents. I also observed the teaching approaches of the congregational rabbis. I wondered about the rabbinic qualities that make for good teaching of adults.

In my second year of graduate studies at the William Davidson Graduate School of Jewish Education at the Jewish Theological Seminary, I took a seminar with Professor Carol Ingall in which the main research assignment was to explore the concept of goodness in teaching. Students selected a teacher we knew and respected as a good teacher. I chose Rabbi and Professor Neil Gillman with whom I had taken two courses at the Seminary. During the research process I began to make connections regarding the questions I had posed earlier about teaching adults, congregational rabbis as teachers of adults, and the excellent teaching I experienced as Rabbi Gillman's student. Fortuitously, not long after I completed the research, the *Journal of Jewish Education* proposed a thematic issue on rabbis, and I published the seminar paper in it. My subsequent research focused on congregational rabbis as teachers of adults. The subject integrated my interest in the nexus between rabbinic identity, adult education, and synagogue communal life. This book grew out of that project.

The more time I spent in the company of the rabbis who participated in my study, the more I began to understand the complexities of their roles as religious educators, communal leaders, and spiritual guides for the adults in their communities. I saw the ways that an emphasis on their clergy identity as teachers shaped not only their teaching, but also the ethos of their synagogues. I viewed close up that while twenty-first-century rabbis share a title with rabbis of previous eras, in many ways who they are and what they do represent a departure from the past rather than a continuation of it.

Certainly, the rabbis in this book continue to transmit the wisdom and truths of Judaism as teachers of Torah. They believe passionately in the holy calling of study as a sacred commitment, as have their predecessors of earlier generations. However, they also confidently articulate an anti-hierarchical and anti-authoritarian stance as rabbinic teachers. Stated positively, they adopt and advance an egalitarian and democratic ethos as members of the American clergy. It would not be an exaggeration to claim that taken together, these latter understandings of both their identity and their role represent a break with tradition rather than an extension of it. In any number of ways, these rabbis embody the capacity of an ancient religious civilization, in this case Judaism, to value the past, live fully in the present, and chart a flourishing future. This is no easy undertaking—and it urgently warrants our attention.

HISTORY

Torah to me is anything that forces you to confront, be in contact with, puts you in touch with the deeper meaning of why we're here . . . Teaching Torah at its best is modeling and empowering people to extract that kind of meaning from their own tradition and to use auxiliary traditions to enlighten it. That's how I try to teach. —Rabbi Eric Miller

The evolution of the contemporary identity of the American congregational rabbi as a teacher of adults grows out of the rich historical tradition of that role. Although the Hebrew word "rabbi" literally translates as "my master" from as early as the first century of the Common Era, the emerging ideology of rabbinic Judaism shaped the image of the rabbi as a teacher, attaching practical and symbolic value to it. Those leaders who influenced the early development of rabbinic Judaism viewed teaching as a sacred activity, grounded in religious devotion, and based upon an obligation to transmit the tradition to current and future generations. In a crucial transformation of Jewish life after the destruction of the Second Temple in seventy CE, for example, teaching Torah was elevated to the equivalent of the offering of priestly sacrifices. Rabbis dared to declare, "A sage's public exposition of Torah was as if he had offered fat and blood [of the biblically prescribed animal sacrifice] on the altar" (Kimelman 1987, 30). Furthermore, according to Moshe Aberbach, talmudic "rabbinical opinion was overwhelmingly opposed to ivory-tower scholarship. To study without imparting knowledge to others was compared to a myrtle in the wilderness whose fragrance was wasted" (1967, 23).

During the long medieval era this conception of the rabbi as teacher gave way to a rabbinic identity founded upon the rabbi's role as interpreter, arbiter, and administrator of Jewish law. Still, even in that time, neither the rabbinic elite nor the masses completely abandoned the idea of the rabbi as a teacher. As Jewish integration advanced in Western Europe and American Jewry established itself in the United States over the course of the nineteenth century, a modern rabbinate reclaimed the primary importance of the rabbi's function as a teacher, along with new obligations, such as pastoral counselor and life-cycle officiant. In a functionalist response to contemporary priorities, these modern rabbis reimagined rabbinic identity to suit the demands of their time. Historian Ismar Schorsch, in describing the new focus on the rabbi as teacher by the rabbinate in Western Europe during the middle of the nineteenth century, wrote:

> [T]he modern rabbi became the primary expositor of Judaism for both children and adults, learned and unlettered Jews, government officials and Christian bystanders. As communal discipline and cohesion waned, he labored to edify, persuade, and inspire indifferent coreligionists by translating venerated texts, concepts, values, and rites into their Western equivalents. School and synagogue became his domain and he spoke in the name of the Bible, the Jewish people, Jewish history, and all of Judaism rather than just the corpus of Jewish law. (1991, 14–15)

Schorsch argued that the conception of the rabbi as teacher in the modern era differs from that held by earlier generations of rabbis who claimed the same title. In the West, at least among modernizing rabbis, a rabbi's primary place for teaching was no longer the *yeshivot* (academies of study). Rather, the synagogue assumed that hallowed designation. Moreover, in referring to the synagogue as the locale where rabbis fulfilled their obligations to the Jewish community, Schorsch explained, "The alliance of rabbi and synagogue was as novel as the roles assigned to each" (1991, 17).

From Schorsch's observations, we may reasonably infer that in spite of the titular connection with earlier ideas about the rabbi as a teacher, the modern synagogue rabbi's role as a teacher represents an identity transformation. The exigencies of modern Jewish and secular culture have contributed to such a change. Rabbis, and those who take a close interest in them, have been examining the responses to these changes in our era. A careful look at writings about rabbis since the end of World War Two reveals a rich trove of essays and articles, both academic and popular, in the Jewish press and in academic Jewish journals that explore the meaning and purpose of rabbinic identity. Publications ranging from *Commentary* and *Tikkun* to *Sh'ma* and the *Journal of Jewish Communal Service* have contributed to the discussion. Academic journals, such as *Conservative Judaism*, the *Journal of Jewish Education*, and *Reform Judaism*, have included essays and research on rabbinic identity. They frequently discussed the extent to which the modern rabbi's identity as a teacher remains, or should remain, an essential component of rabbinic practice. Most offered broad assessments in their characterization of the rabbi as teacher, often prescriptive, with regard to the nature of rabbinic identity. Since 2000 books by the journalists Paul Wilkes (2000) and Stephen Fried (2003) were published that provided insights into the dilemmas and dynamics of the modern rabbinate through the stories of two rabbis and their respective congregations.

A Few Words About Synagogue Adult Jewish Education

In the post-World War Two period, synagogues became the mainstay of adult Jewish education efforts. Teaching adults became the accepted preserve of congregational rabbis. Often the rabbi acted as the only adult educator for members of a synagogue. Even with the creation of new kinds of adult Jewish learning programs and settings, particularly during the 1990s, synagogues stayed the primary location for adults who sought to study. While the rabbi served as the teacher, synagogue-based adult learning was not limited to subjects understood narrowly as religious. In fact, Steven Cohen and Aryeh Davidson, in their work on adult Jewish learning, divided its content into two groups: subjects of a "religious nature," such as "Jewish holidays, prayer, Jewish theology (God), Jewish spirituality, Jewish ritual observance, Hebrew, the Torah or Bible, and the Talmud"; and those that they name "cultural, ethnic, or peoplehood-oriented subjects," such as "Jewish history, art, genealogy, food or cooking, social justice, the Holocaust, Israel, Yiddish, Jewish music, etc" (2001, 21). According to Cohen and Davidsons's distinction, the rabbis you will read about in the following pages engage predominantly, although not exclusively, in teaching religious subjects.

The question, however, of what exactly constitutes religious education in a synagogue remains ambiguous. Jewish tradition views text study as a sacred obligation, as a mitzvah, but adult Jewish educators tend not to explicitly refer to their teaching practice in this manner (Grant et al. 2004). After studying publicity literature describing adult religious education, for example, Lisa Grant and her colleagues identified a linguistic distinction in Jewish and Christian understandings of adult learning. They claimed:

> "[R]eligious education" is a term more frequently connected to Christian circles than to Jewish ones . . . where adult Jewish learning is generally conceptualized as a multidimensional process that can help learners to gain an appreciation of Jewish history, culture, literature, practice and belief. (Grant et al. 2004, 14)

From their perusal of Christian adult religious education literature and studies in the sociology of religion, however, they also observed: ". . . the quest for increased understanding of religious teachings and the desire for greater personal meaning in life may be a strong motivating factor for adults from across the religious spectrum" (ibid.). The rabbis in this book did not speak explicitly about religious education per se, but their practice expressed the idea that teaching adults involved a search for meaning that extended well beyond intellectual curiosity alone. Spiritual and religious exploration consistently animated their interactions with adult learners.

As mentioned above, contemporary rabbis traditionally view adult education as a special focus of their teaching in synagogue settings. They customarily prioritize teaching adults over other age cohorts. In spite of grave concerns in the American Jewish community about the ongoing vitality of synagogues, they continue to function as a primary address for adult Jewish learning. Synagogue rabbis continue to be the go-to educators when adults decide to pursue Jewish learning. As Cohen and Davidson noted:

> How do we explain the popularity of the synagogue as a locus of current Jewish learning in classes and study groups? Aside from all [their] other assets, synagogues are numerous and widely scattered; generally at least one is found very near where most Jews live. Nearly two thirds of American Jews (64%) live within 15 minutes of a synagogue. More than two fifths (41%) live within 10 minutes of one . . . Synagogues are quite accessible, local institutions, often surrounded by concentrated congregants who encounter one another outside the temple, thereby organically reinforcing their bonds of community. (2001, 26–27)

INTRODUCTION

Despite the importance of the synagogue as a center for Jewish education, no comprehensive studies focusing on synagogue rabbis as teachers of adults have been published until now. According to Jack Wertheimer, since the 1990s the American Jewish communal leadership has clamored for solutions to reinvigorate an institution—the synagogue— that they perceive as in dire need of drastic repair (2005, 3). Efforts to do so include initiatives by individual synagogues and by synagogues working in partnership with federations and with national organizations, such as Synagogue 2000 (S2K, now S3K), Synagogue Transformation and Renewal (STAR), and the Experiment in Congregational Learning (ECE), all of which were created explicitly to support "synagogue renewal efforts" (Wertheimer 2005, 64). In this same article, Wertheimer noted two developments highly relevant to my study: Efforts to redefine the roles of the rabbi and the cantor occupied the attention of these groups; and an emphasis on adult study as one of ten common trends across the denominational spectrum appeared prominently as a factor (ibid., 77). Wertheimer's analysis suggests that American Jewish leaders view both the clergy and the adult laity as worthy of focus if the synagogue is to remain essential as a locus of Jewish life.

My subject addresses the characteristics and implications of Wertheimer's trenchant observations through a focus on rabbinic identity. My study catapults rabbis, as members of the American clergy, into a critical discussion not only about why they matter as teachers, but also why they must articulate an inspiring educational vision as spiritual leaders. Furthermore, the thriving of the religious tradition that they love, no less than the flourishing of their congregations, depend on how well they translate that vision into practice.

AN ARGUMENT IN FAVOR OF STUDYING RABBIS

I have an eighty-three-year-old man who comes almost every week to Torah study. He was in the kindertransport.[2] The last time he saw his parents was at his Bar Mitzvah. He has even said to me that he could have been a rabbi. On the one hand, he rejects, because of his experiences, the God who is active in human affairs. At the same time, he cannot get past the literal meaning of the Torah—the notion that the sea really split, that the manna really fell from

---

2. The name given to the rescue mission set up nine months before World War Two began that brought ten thousand Jewish children to the United Kingdom from Nazi Germany, and German-annexed territories between 1938–1940.

heaven—because in his opinion, if God did that, if God could do that, then where was God during the Holocaust for his mom and dad? So he's a little boy in that, but at the same time he's like a little boy in his heart and a grown man in his head. I sit there with him on Shabbat, and he'll sit there on Shabbat saying, "Help me." How do I break through to this person? How do I make a breakthrough? Every so often we do. It's like psychology—somebody has a breakthrough. It's a progression. —Rabbi Jonathan Fisk

Given that the term "rabbi" has undergone many incarnations through its long history, it seems appropriate that at the beginning of this century we turn again to a consideration of its meaning. Already two decades ago Lee Bycel, in his research on rabbinic transformation, asked his readers, "Does the role of the modern rabbi reflect a fundamental shift from that of the rabbi's predecessors, or is it a role based on the same values and principles which guided the earliest rabbis? Does the literal understanding of the rabbi as 'my teacher' still guide the rabbinate?" (1995, 60). Although the three rabbis whose portraits you will read in the following chapters would undoubtedly respond affirmatively to the latter question posed by Bycel, my research leads me to argue that in the United States the concept of rabbi as teacher is critically shaped, both consciously and unconsciously, by the bracing encounter of millennia-old Jewish texts, traditions, and values with the ethos of an American democratic and egalitarian society.

In the Reform synagogues and the one Conservative synagogue described in this book, the Jewish educational orientations of their rabbis often share more in common with the educational philosophies articulated by such scholars as John Dewey and Israel Scheffler than they do with approaches of earlier generations of rabbis who called themselves teachers. This is not a new finding. Historian Jonathan Sarna, in his introduction to an edited work on the history of the American rabbinate across denominational spectrums, wrote, "Functionally speaking they [the rabbis of our time] resemble one another far more than they resemble the traditional *rabbonim* of centuries past" (in Marcus and Peck 1985, 8). If such is the case, and my research does support Sarna's claim, then what implications emerge out of this reality for rabbis? In a culture in which understandings of religious affiliation and identity speedily evolve, not only rabbis, but also clergy more broadly, as well as seminary educators who prepare the clergy, require new knowledge to inform, elevate, and shape the vision and practice that they bring to their work.

INTRODUCTION

Anyone concerned with the position and purpose of clergy who aspire to bring education into the forefront of their work with adults must take bold steps to clearly articulate why clergy continue to matter as educational leaders for American adult populations. If they fail to do so in this "do-it-yourself" hyper-connected world, people will search elsewhere for existential and transcendent wisdom, guidance, and meaning. Clergy will put their own relevance into question. Correspondingly, the capacity for our religious traditions to participate constructively and humanely in any public discourse will inevitably wane. The plurality of religious voices that enrich the common conversations in an open and free society will decline, to the detriment of all. Tragically, we find ample evidence of this trend accelerating, as the more extreme representatives of our religious leadership are often viewed as the only authentic voices in our remarkably diverse religious culture. It is not too late to arrest this movement, but our clergy must clearly affirm that it is possible and desirable.

PORTRAITURE

Chapters 2, 3, and 4 each focus on one of the rabbis in my study. Their identities are protected by giving them, their synagogues, and any other individuals they reference pseudonyms. These three chapters, as well as the remaining four chapters, developed from my research using a social science methodology known as portraiture.[3] I named the rabbis Jonathan Fisk, Rina Lewin, and Eric Miller, identified subsequently by first name, as I addressed them in our interviews and correspondence. Between 2007 and 2009 I conducted research with them. Over a fourteen-month period I concluded three semi-structured ninety-minute interviews with each one separately at their synagogues. Several e-mail exchanges followed the interviews. I also spoke informally with a random selection of their adult learners. Finally, I attended their study groups, classes, and many worship services over a period of several months of observation at each of their synagogues. While two of the three rabbis referred to retreats, trips, and pastoral counseling as additional settings for teaching, I limited my time to

---

3. The pseudonyms protect the identity of the rabbis, their synagogues, and anyone else they refer to in their interviews. I provided the rabbis with a consent letter that described the research project and their part in it. See Appendix A for a template. See the following website for further information on human subjects, qualitative research, and ethnography: http://www.nsf.gov/bfa/dias/policy/human.jsp.

places within the synagogue itself or in nearby offsite locations, such as in the rabbi's home. These were accessible and feasible for me to attend over an extended period of time both financially and time-wise (See Appendix B for further description of the method).

The three rabbis worked in the same geographic area with a large population of college-educated congregants. Their midsized synagogues of between five hundred and six hundred fifty households were located outside a major metropolis with ample resources for Jewish life. These rabbis repeatedly surfaced in my inquiries with Jewish leaders and laity regarding outstanding rabbinic educators of adults; the three also were willing to meet with me over an extended period of time. Research involving rabbis who work in different Jewish milieus may lead to additional or different findings.

Portraiture is a well-established form of educational research. Credit for this distinctive kind of qualitative methodology in education must go to Sara Lawrence-Lightfoot, a sociologist and now emeritus professor at Harvard's Graduate School of Education. She pioneered the approach in the 1980s, innovatively integrating ethnography and biography to create a unique kind of scholarly writing (1983; 1997). Each of the portrait chapters follows a similar structure: I begin by introducing the synagogue context and then move on to pertinent biographical background. I describe and analyze the significant themes in the rabbi's perception of his or her identity as a teacher. These portraits draw from the interviews, observations, writings, and e-mail correspondence.

Portraiture suits my topic. It emphasizes the fundamental and generative importance of the perception, beliefs, attitudes, and experiences of the participants. In order to build a holistic understanding of the rabbis' identities as teachers, I needed to hear about who they were as people beyond their functional roles in the synagogue. A phrase sometimes affirmed by educators—"We teach who we are"—seemed to apply even more in the case of rabbis, given the potentially powerful influence of their clergy personas. As a consequence, the accompanying portraits benefit substantially from the open-ended, in-depth interviews that characterize the portraiture process. They include background regarding the rabbis' formative experiences since childhood that have implications for their rabbinic selves. The interviews enabled me to explore the interconnections among biography, philosophy, and education.

Introduction

In line with ethnographic methods drawn from anthropology and sociology, portraiture emphasizes the necessity of situating the research subjects contextually. As a participant-observer at each of the rabbis' synagogues for several months at a time, I became part of the social and cultural milieus. Attendance gave me the chance to interact with their congregants, albeit as a person whom they knew occupied a particular position as rabbinic researcher. The conversations and informal interviews with congregants helped flesh out and deepen my understanding of the rabbis from the vantage point of their learners.

Portraiture and Grounded Theory

Portraiture also shares qualities with grounded theory, another approach to qualitative research. Kathy Charmaz defined grounded theory as "a method of conducting qualitative research that focuses on creating conceptual frameworks or theories through building inductive analysis from the data. Hence, analytic categories are directly 'grounded' in the data" (Charmaz 2006, 187). Grounded theory is based on the inductive "constant comparative method" described by Glaser and Straus (1967) in which data are compared with each other, categories are developed from the data, the categories are compared with each other, and these comparisons, in turn, generate concepts and eventually theories out of the categories (Charmaz 2006; Merriam 2009). Following this trajectory, I used the transcripts of my interviews and my field notes to develop emergent themes (also called categories) for each rabbi. These themes included the following tags:

- Rabbi Rina Lewin: Connection; Creativity and creation; Integration; Sharing/Co-learning
- Rabbi Jonathan Fisk: Inquiry; Connection; Discovery; Learning; Loving Judaism; Sharing knowledge
- Rabbi Eric Miller: Creative ambiguity; Keeping an open mind; Learning; Modeling how to think; Process teaching; Scholarship; Teaching Torah

For each of these I then wrote memos exploring their implications, reflecting on them, and fleshing out my impressions in light of the research questions. The memos helped to identify gaps in my data and to recognize areas that needed further attention.

I also shared the transcripts and coding with colleagues in order to solicit feedback about my logic, methods, or biases, and to establish credibility. Organizing categories for each rabbi emerged as a result of this step-by-step process. These categories became the basis for the findings in each portrait chapter. Finally, I synthesized the results in the domains of teaching approaches, teaching style, and teaching aims to provide an overarching analysis of the rabbi's role as a teacher of adults. This way of integrating the research affirms Lawrence-Lightfoot's insight: "The process of creating a whole often feels like weaving a tapestry or piecing together a quilt" (Lawrence-Lightfoot and Davis 1997, 12).

SCHOLARSHIP ON ADULT EDUCATION AND ADULT JEWISH EDUCATION

My topic developed out of research in the academic fields of adult religious education, adult education, adult learning, and adult Jewish education. Scholarship on faith formation, religious identity, and spiritual development also informed the research. Chapter 1 addresses the foundational theories and the scholarship that they have stimulated. The book's subject matter purposely invites conversations with clergy, adult religious educators, and seminary educators from all religious orientations who seek to understand the dynamics of clergy identity and adult education in their religious communities. As the authors of *Educating Clergy: Teaching Practices and Pastoral Imagination* discovered, shared concerns among Christian and Jewish seminaries about how to best prepare their seminarians for clergy positions in twenty-first-century America provide a persuasive rationale for the benefits of this study to Christian populations (Foster et al., 2006).

The following questions initiated and propelled my research:

- *What is the role of the congregational rabbi as a teacher of adults?*
- *What do congregational rabbis consider good teaching of adults?*
- *In what ways do congregational rabbis represent a distinct category of adult educators?*

Some confusion exists even in academic circles regarding the description and definition of adult education. To avoid such confusion in this book, I drew on a definition proposed by Sharan Merriam and Ralph Brockett. They described adult education as "activities intentionally designed for the purpose of bringing about learning among those whose age, social roles, or self-perception define them as adults" (1997, 8).

While rabbis often call themselves teachers, all activities of a congregational rabbi are not construed in this book as instances of educational activity. The notion that adult education is an intentionally purposeful activity is important to the context of the congregational rabbi's identity as a teacher. Rabbis inhabit many roles, including teacher, pastor, preacher, and life-cycle officiant. Although teaching enters into each role in different ways, the rabbis attempted to differentiate instances of teaching in the latter three from the more intentional efforts in formal learning settings. In fact, an awareness of role differentiation in the various settings within which the rabbis function in their congregations emerged as a key component of how they approached their interactions with learners.

While scholarship in education often remains secluded within academia, rather than moving out into the larger world of educational practice, portraiture aims at overcoming that distance. "The power of portraiture . . . lies in its explicitly humanistic impulse. It embraces both analytic rigor (a perspective that is distant, discerning, and skeptical) and community building (acts of intimacy and connection)" (Lawrence-Lightfoot and Davis 1997, 10). Thoroughly grounded in a scholarly approach to the subject, I believe this book exemplifies Sara Lawrence-Lightfoot's aspirations for portraiture. My hope is that it finds a readership that includes clergy, seminary educators, adult religious educators, and lay leaders of all faiths who care about the religious and spiritual lives of adults.

THE BOOK'S CHAPTERS

Chapter 1 provides an overview of the field's foundational literature, while crucially introducing new directions for theory construction based on my work. The three portrait chapters follow. The title of each of the portrait chapters speaks to an aspect of the rabbis' teacher identity that is central to their self-understanding. The three findings chapters present an analysis and synthesis of my research. Three organizing categories structure each of these chapters: rabbis as facilitators, co-learners, and community builders. These constructs emerged organically through the coding of the interviews and observations. Aspects of the theories about adult learning and adult Jewish learning helped contextualize these categories. They are not to be interpreted as prescriptive, in the sense that good clergy teaching must always reflect them. Instead, consistent with the theory of portraiture, they are best understood as a means of generating fruitful concepts for further research about clergy educator identities and roles. More broadly, they invite interreligious conversations about clergy identity and religious education in contemporary society.

Neither do the categories of facilitator, co-learner, and community builder reflect a hierarchy of importance. Instead, they represent a move from an exploration of teaching approaches (facilitation) toward teaching style (co-learner) and, finally, to teaching aims (community building). The approaches, styles, and aims each express particular aspects of the congregational rabbi's identity as a teacher of adults, while taken together they constitute a complex whole.

At the conclusion of each findings chapter, I include a short list of reflective questions for clergy, seminary educators, and any other adult religious educators to consider in light of their own practice and in conversation with the issues addressed. These questions could be used as the basis for journaling, peer learning, mentor-peer coaching, professional learning, or informal dialogue with colleagues. They invite readers to delve into their own identities and beliefs about teaching adults. They give readers a chance to step back from their practice in a nonjudgmental manner and to learn more about who they aspire to be and become as adult religious educators.

The concluding chapter suggests implications for practice and new research, and presents further directions for interreligious collaboration around the subject.

NARRATIVE, TRANSFORMATION, AND SPIRITUALITY

Over the course of writing and revising, I gained valuable feedback from a few insightful readers. They generously pointed out that a distinctive triad composed of three powerful themes appeared as a consistent refrain throughout the portraits and the findings that derive from them. They characterized these three as narrative, transformation, and spirituality. As the next chapter reveals, scholarship in adult education and adult Jewish learning addresses each of them in one way or another to a greater or lesser degree. Metaphorically, narrative, transformation, and spirituality are imagined in the chapters that follow as a constellation. The book demonstrates how the constellation acts as a holistically unifying force in our rabbis' work with adult learners. For those of us who take seriously

INTRODUCTION

a religious tradition and its transformative influence on the wider public world and in our private lives, this book ultimately is about trying to live out the constellation.

Why This Book Matters

The following chapters explore the identity of the contemporary congregational rabbi as a teacher, and more specifically as a teacher of adults. Yet it especially contributes to and seeks to further stimulate a vital discussion about clergy identity in contemporary American religious life. How the three rabbis perceive themselves and their practice of teaching adults acts as a frame within which new insights germinate about broader interreligious concerns. Although no longer the sole representatives of American Jewry, rabbis continue to function as Jewish leaders both within Jewish communities, in their relations with other religious groups, and in American society writ large.

As many of the articles and essays about rabbis show, whether implicitly or explicitly, rabbinic identity is in a place of profound flux. Disputes between Diaspora Jews and the State of Israel regarding the authenticity of rabbinic authority are only one facet of this fluidity, ambiguity, and struggle. With women rabbis, and more recently gays and lesbians being ordained by all of the liberal movements, unavoidable confrontations with millennium-old images and definitions of Jewish clergy are a natural outgrowth of these innovations. But this flux is not unique to Jewish clergy. In the Christian world debates also rage about the legitimacy and identity of the clergy. These arguments often are very public in nature. How are clergy and concerned adults to make sense of these battles?

In a society where information is literally at everyone's fingertips and autonomy is a treasured aspect of an individual's existence, what place remains for clergy who want teaching and learning to be at the core of who they are and what they do? What kind of teaching? What kind of learning? In a culture where spiritual seeking is prioritized over religious practice, why necessarily turn to a member of the clergy for spiritual guidance? What do adults expect of clergy in the way of spiritual inspiration and edification? As a group that is entrusted with transmission of a religious tradition, how are clergy to respond to the ambivalences, confusions, and journeys of contemporary adults who are willing still to look to religious faith and religious culture as a source of wisdom? How are clergy to initiate conversations that respect the multiplicity of voices from the adults they encounter while still calling on the font of knowledge that they posses as clergy? How do their identities as *teachers,* a word fraught with much ambiguity at best in American culture, enrich and uplift? Indeed, a thread that runs throughout the book is the need for clergy to talk less and listen more, an idea that may go against common stereotypes, not to mention practices. This book seeks to provide answers to some of these complex queries. It also is a rallying call to build conversational bridges with people of all faiths who care about the role of religious leadership and religious education in American culture.

chapter 1

FOUNDATIONAL THEORIES AND NEW ADVANCES

What images surface to describe rabbis as teachers of adults? There are, no doubt, many stereotypical characterizations. The question itself invites us to wonder how clergy perceive their identity and their role in relation to the adults in their congregations. It is adults that constitute the majority of their members. Moreover, it is through interactions with adults that the overall spiritual, religious, communal, and financial thriving of their congregations primarily depend. Surprisingly, those of us who care about these clergy and their congregations know very little about how they understand their relationships with adults from an educational perspective.

As recent survey after survey by the Pew Research Center reveals, American adults turn less and less to organized communal religious life. What changes must clergy initiate to reverse this trend? There is urgency to this question. To help our religious and spiritual leaders acquire greater coherence, insight, and direction in response to the needs, yearnings, and interests of adults in the twenty-first century, why not turn to what scholars already know? This chapter addresses the foundational theories in adult education, adult learning, adult religious education, and adult Jewish education. As with all scholarly fields, they provided referential conceptual frameworks during the research process. In turn, my subject advances the knowledge base in new and vital ways by studying rabbis as a cohort of adult religious educators. They possess a distinctive and compelling vision of themselves and their work that demands our sustained attention.

Adult Jewish education is a very recent arrival to the broader academic field of adult education. In the 1990s a small cadre of scholars began publishing their research. Much work remains to be done. To a great extent, scholarship in adult Jewish education relies on theories and research in general adult education. Therefore, it is useful to begin with a broader overview of the latter field. In the first section of the chapter I will address theory construction in adult education. Scholarship here has concentrated mostly on adult learners and on identifying and understanding adult learning processes, rather than on teachers and teaching processes. How do teachers of adults stimulate adult learning? How do they focus and organize their teaching? In the case of religious educators, how is that teaching faithful to a religious tradition?

The relative lack of empirical research around these key questions may be one of the reasons why no major studies focusing on the role of the rabbi, or on the congregational rabbi as a teacher of adults, have yet been published.[1] While the literature on adult education has concentrated on the learner and the learning process, it nonetheless provides some valuable theoretical insights and concepts pertaining to the teacher. These insights and concepts will be highlighted in the latter half of the chapter. Many are directly relevant to the primary concerns of this book.

Yet how many seminaries, Jewish or Christian, devote substantial time in their curriculum to a focused study of adult educational theory and practice? How many of our clergy leave seminary with a secure knowledge base regarding adult learners' intellectual, religious, spiritual, or developmental needs? The answer to those questions, based on my research and a review of the extant literature (such as it exists), is that very few do.

ADULT EDUCATION

The scholarly study of adult education as an academic discipline is less than a century old. In the United States researchers cited 1926 as its founding year (Imel 1989, 134). This date marked the creation of the American Association for Adult Education (AAAE) and along with it systematic efforts to define adult education as a distinct area of professional practice and academic research. Current challenges to the field involve the sheer number of learning theories, as well as their complexity and heterogeneity. As described by Deshler and Hagan (1989), efforts to build theory in adult education often have employed diverse conceptual frameworks. These

---

1. I have published two articles on the subject, sections of which appear in this book. See the Bibliography.

include: integrating theory from other disciplines, most notably psychology; generating theory particular to adult learning and development; and building on critical theory. The three areas provide valuable touchstones in the context of my subject and are addressed in the following sections.

Adult Education and Psychology

Since its inception, adult education theory has been shaped by the discipline of psychology. In particular, psychological research related to adult development has been prominent (Clark and Caffarella 1999, 5). M. Carolyn Clark and Rosemary Caffarella (1999) noted that the idea of adulthood as a developmental construct emerged only in the twentieth century. While the relationship of psychology-generated developmental theories and adult learning theory has its critics (Reeves 1999; Tennant 2002), several conceptual models that grew out of the interaction have been influential and merit further discussion. Prominent among these are Malcolm Knowles's andragogy; theories informed by critical theory, such as transformational learning; and, more recently, narrative development theories. Andragogy, for example, built upon concepts that reflected the influence of sequential psychosocial models of adult development. In contrast, transformational learning and the related concept of perspective transformation grew out of theories of cognitive development. Narrative development, a relative newcomer to the field, drew on theories of personality psychology while postulating an integrated view of the adult's evolving self (McAdams 2001).

Andragogy

Outside the world of academic research in adult learning, the term "andragogy" is practically unknown. Yet andragogy, characterized broadly as "the practice of helping adults earn" (Deshler and Hagan 1989, 155) originated in Europe in the nineteenth century (Knowles 1980). In the 1920s the German social scientist Eugene Rosenstock proposed that adult education required a special group of teachers, methods, and philosophy. He used the term "andragogy" to differentiate it from pedagogy (Knowles 1984, 50). Eduard C. Lindeman, one of the American pioneers of adult education, introduced andragogy as a concept in the United States in the 1920s (Brookfield 1986). But it was Malcom Knowles's (1973/1984, 1980) research on the concept that established andragogy as a dominant, widely disseminated model for applied theory and practice since the 1970s. Knowles incorporated John Dewey's philosophical conceptualization of the educational process, as well as Carl Rogers's (1969) and, to a lesser extent, Abraham Maslow's (1970) psychological theories of adult development.

The essential idea animating andragogy was the claim that adults were developmentally different from children and adolescents. Consequently, adults manifested distinctive qualities as learners that needed to be taken into account in any learning environment. Knowles argued against the behaviorist paradigm espoused by B. F. Skinner and Edward Thorndike that had dominated approaches to learning theory in the United States since the 1950s. Instead, he turned to humanistic psychological theories, claiming that they were better suited developmentally to adults. Whereas in behaviorist models learning was defined in stimulus-response terms as a change in behavior, measurable and exterior to the learner, Knowles emphasized psychological concepts that designated learning as primarily an internal process (Pratt 1993, 16).

Debates About Andragogy

Knowles's articulation of andragogy roused continuing controversy about whether it was intended as a theory of learning, a guide for practice, or a method for teaching. In response to criticism that many of his insights about adult learning could be applied to pre-adult populations, Knowles modified his construct. In later writings he acknowledged that rather than seeing adult learning in sharp distinction to that of children and adolescents, it also was possible to apply aspects of andragogy to these populations.

Andragogy, whether conceived of as theory, model, program, practice, or a set of assumptions, has been critiqued further for generalizing about all adults as self-directed learners. Critics claimed that it had become an ideologically prescriptive construct that ignored societal factors (Brookfield 1986; Pratt 1993). Moreover, Daniel Pratt questioned whether embedded in andragogy was a philosophical stance, whereby the focus on the learner's autonomy and self-direction reflected the values of an American middle-class, democratic society (Pratt 1993, 22). Given these debates, it was only a matter of time before new theoretical constructs emerged to challenge andragogy's dominance.

ADULT LEARNING BUILDS ON CRITICAL THEORY

As mentioned previously, significant criticism of andragogy concerned its indifference to the power of societal context and ideology in adult education. By the 1970s, even as andragogy's prominence continued, a trend toward applying critical theory also emerged. Paolo Freire's influential *Pedagogy of the Oppressed* (1971) reflected a focus on the emancipatory possibilities of adult education; its claims overlapped with research into critical theory as a context for examining adult learning. Beginning in the late 1990s, the number of articles on adult education theory that employed critical theory as a framework of analysis and interpretation has surpassed the number of articles on andragogy (Merriam et al. 2007).

Critical theory grew out of the sociological and philosophical ideas of the Frankfurt School in Germany in the 1920s, and subsequently in North America. It emerged as a way "to find a clue to understand the nature of society and the dynamics of ideological, cultural, and psychic domination" (Deshler and Hagan 1989, 155). North American theorists of adult education working within a framework of critical theory, such as Stephen Brookfield (1986; 1995; 2005; 2006), Patricia Cranton (2000; 2006), and Jack Mezirow (1981; 1985; 1995; 2000) argued that adult education should center on the ability of adults to cognitively reflect on the interaction between self and society. They viewed the aim of adult education as actualizing the ability of adults to engage in reflective thinking. The overarching goal was "human liberation and empowerment" (Deshler and Hagan 1989, 155).

Conceptualizing adult education via critical theory placed the emphasis on the learning process as an internal act linked to changes in perception, attitudes, beliefs and, ultimately, behavior. From this perspective, critical theory did not imagine education as a process of transmission of information from expert to novice. Instead, it sought to understand the processes through which the teaching-learning transaction enabled adults to critically reflect on the knowledge base and assumptions that underlay and informed their attitudes, beliefs, and behaviors.

Transformational Learning Theory

In the American context, critical theory in adult education established its mark through transformational learning theory. Jack Mezirow's (1981; 1985; 1990; 2000) application of critical theory shaped the field substantially. Mezirow's initial empirical research in adult education was with middle-class, college-educated women and drew on the work of the German critical theorist Jürgen Habermas. He cited Habermas's two domains of learning that have "different purposes, logics of inquiry, criteria of rationality, and modes of validating belief" (Mezirow 2000, 8): *Instrumental learning* involved the way that people control their environment and other individuals, while *communicative learning* involved figuring out what people intend when they communicate with each other. Communicative learning usually focused on "feelings, intentions, values, and moral issues" (ibid.). Mezirow claimed that learning usually included aspects of both instrumental and communicative learning. Both can and should lead to what he labeled as transformative learning, reformulating Habermas's third domain, *emancipatory learning*.

In his ongoing scholarship, Mezirow has endeavored to elucidate the core aspects of transformational learning. He identified what he called "frames of reference" that included "the structure of assumptions and expectations through which we filter sense impressions." The frames of reference, also identified as "meaning perspectives," are formed unconsciously (ibid., 16). According to Mezirow, "Learning occurs in one of four ways: by elaborating existing frames of reference, by learning new frames of reference, by transforming points of view, or by transforming habits of mind" (ibid., 19). Perspective transformation, a key component of transformational learning theory, was the primary outcome of being able to critically evaluate the frames of reference that guide an individual (ibid., 18).

Robert Kegan, a prominent theoretician of adult education and its relation to cognitive psychology and constructive-developmental theory, proposed that transformational learning theory was particularly suited to the developmental needs of adults in the twenty-first century (2000). Kegan used his constructive-developmental theory to chart the evolution of adult thinking and the influence of formal learning in relation to the complexity of contemporary society (1982; 1994; 2000). According to Kegan, the particular stressors of contemporary existence require that adults develop the cognitive capacity to make autonomous decisions about where to place their loyalties when confronted with the often bewildering and relativistic possibilities of modern society. Nevertheless, adults need equally to achieve cognitive distance from those same choices in order to understand the reasoning behind them.

As a lifespan-developmental psychologist, Kegan presented a phased model of adults moving from concrete thinking, to abstraction, to abstract systems, and ultimately to dialectical thinking that incorporated paradox and contradiction. His theory integrated psychological and contextual models in an effort to analyze how adults mentally make sense of the complexity of their world.

New Perspectives on Transformational Learning Theory

Transformational learning theory generated a multiplicity of research paradigms and empirically data-driven research. As may be expected with such a dominant model, it also garnered criticism. Mezirow's original framework was critiqued for being overly cognitive in orientation, ignoring a more holistic understanding of the learner that included emotions (Dirkx 2006; 2012). Daniele D. Flannery and Elizabeth Hayes argued that transformative learning theory needed to encompass not only the cognitive, but also the "spiritual, emotional, intuitive, and other embodied dimensions" of the learners' experiences (2001, 37).

In response to and alongside these critiques, new interpretations of transformational learning have emerged since 2000. In 2012 editors Edward W. Taylor and Patricia Cranton published *The Handbook of Transformative Learning: Theory, Research, and Practice*. This book's rich collection of essays provided a comprehensive view of more recent scholarship. It broadened the discussion of transformational learning theory to include new areas of inquiry, such as the influence of relationships, spirituality, emotions, narrative, cross-cultural perspectives, and informal educational settings. Earlier, in 2008, Taylor wrote about the internal contradictions in the various interpretations of transformational learning theory. In particular he addressed the aims of transformation as alternating between predominantly personal, primarily societal, or in tandem with each other (2008, 12). In a review of the literature in the *Handbook*, however, he and co-author Melissa J. Snyder provided a description of transformative learning that captured an essential dimension of the spirit of new research directions. They explained:

> Transformative learning is found at the intersection between the personal and the social, where a transformation is a reciprocal process (Scott 2003)—a product both of others (social recognition, relationships) and of personal change—which potentially leads to a greater sense of individual responsibility for and about

> others (social accountability). This sense of social accountability seems to indicate a moral outcome associated with transformative learning, possibly reflective of greater empathy. (49)

Based on the research presented in the *Handbook*, it becomes clear that the field of transformational learning theory continues to deepen and broaden its research scope and findings.

NARRATIVE DEVELOPMENT AND NARRATIVE LEARNING

The fields of literature, linguistics, gender studies, and other related disciplines in the humanities and social sciences have explored narrative for decades; adult education, in contrast, was a latecomer to this realm. Yet late twentieth-century and early twenty-first-century American culture expends tremendous energy on pushing individuals and groups to tell their stories. To ignore this trend is to be oblivious to powerful societal currents (Carey 2007). Researchers at the intersection of psychology and neuroscience continue to make new discoveries about memory, narrative, and the life course. In the 1990s scholars in the field of adult learning started to focus on the links between theories of narrative and adult education. In part the turn to narrative reflected the consensus in the field regarding the primary importance of the concept of experience to adult learning (Clark and Rossiter, 2008, 63–64).

The authors of the 2007 *Learning in Adulthood: A Comprehensive Guide* offered a definition of narrative based on their analysis of its relationship to diverse theories of adult learning: "Narrative learning is the use of stories in the construction of meaning, whether the meaning-making has to do with the self, with the content of instruction, or with the world around us" (2007, 216). Marsha Rossiter, a leading theoretician of the application of narrative developmental theory to adult education noted that the interaction of narrative development and adult learning "looks at the storied nature of development and considers story as a metaphor for human life" (1999, 59). Citing research by Donald Polkinghorne and Jerome Bruner, she argued, "A narrative understanding of adult development is grounded in the assumption that narrative is a primary structure though which human beings organize and make meaning of their experience" (1999a, 78).

Scholars who work at the intersection of psychology and other fields of inquiry have influenced adult education research on narrative.

Polkinghorne (1988) and Dan McAdams (1993; 2001; 2005) constructed substantial theoretical and empirical frameworks for applying narrative knowing and narrative development to adult learning. Rossiter (1999; 1999a; 2002) and Rossiter and Clark (2007; 2008) contributed prominently to establishing a foundation for understanding the conceptual interaction between adult education and narrative. They assessed the importance of narrative learning in adulthood in the following way:

> As learners become sensitized to the narrative nature of experience, they also begin to recognize that they are themselves both constituted by narratives and situated within multiple narratives as individuals, families, organizations, cultures, and societies. The recognition of this narrative situatedness creates the possibility for critique, for the questioning of underlying assumptions . . . (2007, 70)

Narrative theories challenged the sequential phase and stage development claims embedded in both andragogy and transformational learning theory. Their proponents have argued that development is as much, if not more so, a highly individual and internally driven process of self-perception and growth. They offered an integrated and holistic understanding of research into adult development. In this way they provided a bridge to the next area of focus: spirituality, religion, and faith in adult education. The scholarly study of adult education historically avoided these three domains. Yet, slowly, researchers are increasingly giving attention to them. As with adult education generally, scholarship tends to focus on the learners more than on the educators.

SPIRITUALITY

Spirituality is an increasingly familiar if diffuse concept in American society. From statistics in various Pew Reports about the decline of formal religious affiliation among adult Americans, to the growing interest in Eastern forms of spiritual practice, such as meditation and yoga, scholars in adult education can no longer ignore these complex cultural developments. In 2000 the journal *New Directions for Adult and Continuing Education* devoted an entire issue to essays on spirituality and adult learning. The editors and authors acknowledged the difficulty in finding consensus around the term "spirituality" itself. But, because, "like dandelions in the spring, the term is cropping up everywhere," the editors maintained that adult educators needed to address it. They asserted:

> Adult educators have paid a great deal of attention to the aesthetic, social, emotional, physical, intellectual, and other aspects of education but have neglected the equally important spiritual dimension. We argue that to omit the spiritual dimension is to ignore the importance of a holistic approach to adult learning as well as the complexity of the adult learner. (English and Gillen 2000, 2)

The editors also indicated a variety of longstanding structural and ideological obstacles to incorporating spirituality into adult education programs (2000, 85). Elizabeth Tisdell, however, cited the "implicit" influence of spirituality historically on the field of adult education, in particular through the actions of social justice adult educators (2008, 29). She also argued for a distinction between spirituality and religion, while acknowledging the potentially formative influence of religion in an individual's spiritual evolution. She claimed that conflation of the terms "spirituality" and "religion" was a primary reason for confusion about the two concepts:

> But if one remembers that spirituality is primarily about an individual's experience whereas religion is about an organized community of faith, it's possible to glean whether an author is really talking about religion or spirituality. (2008, 29)

These voices join with other efforts to bring spirituality into the realm of adult education. No discussion of the subject would be complete without reference to the influence of author and educator Parker Palmer. Although his work does not contribute to the corpus of academic research, understood narrowly, his extensive exploration of spirituality among adults, and with clergy and educators in particular, warrants attention. Through his prolific publications and through the creation of the Center for Courage and Renewal, Palmer has encouraged adult educators of all backgrounds to honestly, passionately, and collaboratively examine the relationship of spirituality, teaching, and learning.

RELIGION, FAITH DEVELOPMENT THEORY, AND ADULT EDUCATION

One of the primary difficulties in addressing religious and faith development in adult education concerns finding the proper balance between any kind of universal claims about religion and faith and acknowledging the qualities of particular religions. This reality may be among the reasons why education scholars have shied away from attempts at such research. Recently, a volume of the journal *New Directions for Adult and Continuing Education* devoted an entire issue to the subject (2012). Even there, however, the tension between particularistic and universal orientations was evident through the selection of essays. Historically, an early collection of essays edited by Nancy T. Foltz, the *Handbook of Adult Religious Education*, attempted to broadly tackle the subject (1986). The book explored adult religious development and education from the perspective of age cohorts, such as young adults, middle-aged adults, and older adults. It also approached the subject by addressing such groups as separated and divorced adults and single parents. The collection included recommendations regarding the different developmental needs of these groups. Another valuable effort was Catholic scholar and educator John Elias's *The Foundations and Practice of Adult Religious Education* (1993), which sought to integrate philosophy of education, adult education, and adult religious education.

Two authors who wrote about adult religious education mostly for Christian contexts have contributed more generally to the discussion about its practices and its aims. One of these is Leon McKenzie. His 1982 book, *The Religious Education of Adults*, (updated in 2002 with the participation of R. Michael Harton), derived its argument from theories of adult development and adult learning. McKenzie focused primarily on adult education in Christian communities. He delivered a strong attack on the ineffectiveness of such endeavors in churches. He claimed, moreover, that applying the principles of adult learning theory would help remedy the existing failures. Linda Vogel's *Religious Education of Older Adults* (1983) also embraced developmental theory to understand the particular needs of older adults. Her *Teaching and Learning in Communities of Faith: Empowering Adults through Religious Education* (1991) used journey metaphors to consider adult models for learning in a communal setting. The book blended theory and practice to examine how adult learning builds faith in religious community. In both of her books, Vogel, a former professor and scholar of Christian education, tried to balance her rootedness in Christianity with an attentiveness to the themes in her work that transcended any particular religious tradition. Like Foltz and McKenzie, she encouraged practitioners to incorporate theory from general adult educational research as an avenue toward improving adult religious education practice.

Christian scholar Dwayne Huebner, whose work has reached a wide audience, also deserves attention. Huebner warned against theories of religious education that depended too heavily on secular education scholarship, in particular, psychological theories of development. He believed that such an approach inhibited the generation of theories distinctively relevant to religious education. According to George Brown Jr., part of Huebner's critique of American religious education concerned the emphasis on individualism. In contrast, Huebner sought a "more communal and covenantal understanding of education" (Brown "Contributions"). In *The Lure of the Transcendent* Huebner claimed, "The question that educators need to ask is not how people learn and develop, but what gets in the way of the great journey—the journey of the self or soul. Education is a way of attending to and caring for that journey" (1999, 405). Huebner's influence in adult religious education was due especially to his collaboration with faculty and students at Teachers College, Union Theological Seminary (where he worked for many years), and the Jewish Theological Seminary. In that capacity he taught alongside and mentored a number of individuals who went on to important positions in higher education and seminary education, such as Michael Apple at the University of Wisconsin, Mary Boys at Union Theological Seminary, and Joseph Lukinsky at the Jewish Theological Seminary.

Adult religious education has produced several valuable works and some important thinkers, but faith development theory is another entryway into spirituality and religion. Educators and scholars alike recognize James Fowler's work. His 1981 *Stages of Faith* has been as an enduring influence (Dykstra 1986, 250, 268). Fowler's theory deserves attention from adult education scholars and practitioners alike. As he wrote: "Some of the most interesting and powerful faith stage transitions occur only in adulthood. Faith, as seen here, involves an ongoing process, of forming and reforming our ways of being in and seeing the world" (1986, 37). Craig Dykstra maintained that Fowler's faith development theory encourages religious educators to engage in conversations regarding adult religious education's aims, processes, and participants (1986). While the work of Sharon Daloz Parks has added new dimensions to faith development theory (1991; 2011), overall the concept has not stimulated a process of ongoing research in adult education. Fowler seems to be a unique scholarly voice.

Faith development theory also received its share of criticism from a variety of research perspectives. Fowler's critics argued that his theory failed to convincingly differentiate its claims about faith from overall processes of human development. Feminists also critiqued the metaphors Fowler employed to describe faith (Dykstra and Parks 1986, 9). Such debates suggested that faith development required ongoing scholarly research, both empirical and theoretical, before affirming any definitive claims about its enduring scholarly legitimacy. Moreover, its application to adult learning needs further refining; its sequential premise puts it at odds to some degree with recent findings related to themes emerging about narrative development theory and the adult lifespan.

FROM THE ADULT LEARNER TO THE TEACHER OF ADULTS

As previously discussed, theory construction in adult education has concentrated heavily on identifying adult learning processes. The reasons for this focus are not clear but may be linked to the philosophical orientations of researchers and practitioners (Elias and Merriam 1980). Thus, concepts related to the teaching of adults tended to be derivative, dependent on the findings about learning among adult populations. In other words, theories in adult education about the role of the teacher and teaching practice usually grew out of learning theories rather than vice versa. This orientation notwithstanding, the literature provides some theoretical insights that bear directly on the central question of this book, namely, the role of rabbis as teachers of adults. For this reason, the following section will revisit some of the major approaches discussed above with an eye for what they reveal about the role of the teacher.

Andragogy and the Role of the Teacher

Andragogy rejected the hierarchical understanding of the teacher as an expert or authority figure. Knowles built on the value he attached to the concept of experience, as well as on Rogers's psychological theories (1969) about the centrality of the teacher-learner relationship to adult education. As a consequence, he described the "art of teaching" as the ability to "create a rich environment from which students can extract learning and then to guide their interaction with it so as to optimize their learning from it" (1980, 56). The responsibility for learning shifted from teachers determining what the student should know to aiding students as they figured out the focus of their learning (1980, 56). Knowles, like Rogers, identified the teacher's preferred role as that of facilitator, stressing the personal relationship established between the teacher and the learner as critical to the educational exchange (1980, 75). He emphasized the teacher's position as someone who helped support the learner's overall flourishing as a human being.

Knowles's use of the term "facilitator" invites description. He saw it as a set of personality traits essential to the role of the teacher of adults: "Realness or genuineness, non-possessive caring, prizing, trust, and respect, and empathic understanding and sensitive and accurate listening" (Knowles, citing Rogers, 1984, 76). The facilitator focused on collaboration with the adult learners in the learning process. A strong emphasis on discussion predominated in such settings, rather than the pursuit of a predetermined transmission of content from the expert to the novice through lectures. Facilitation involved a high level of mutual communication between teacher and learner about the means and the ends of learning (Langenbach 1988, 171). Knowles asserted that the goal of the facilitator was "to develop a total environment conducive to human growth and self-actualization; to create an educative society" (1980, 38).

Andragogy's notion of the teacher as a facilitator implied a shift in conception about the authority of the teacher. The teacher must demonstrate confidence that the learners will take responsibility for their learning; the teacher must recognize the centrality of the learners' experiences and their development as independent persons as key to the learning (Elias and Merriam 1979, 128). Jane Vella, author of numerous books on the intersection of adult learning and the teaching of adults (2000; 2002; 2007), and founder of a center dedicated to adult learning (Global Learning Partners) developed her theory of dialogue education in conversation with Knowles's concepts. Her ideas about facilitation blended Knowles's and Freire's understandings of emancipatory education. To Vella, andragogy was not at odds with critical theory. Rather, they depended on each other. Adult educators benefited from understanding both constructs.

Transformational Learning Theory and the Role of the Teacher

As in the case of andragogy, scholars of transformational learning theory proposed an anti-hierarchical interaction between teacher and adult learner. Teachers were expected to engage in a process of critical reflection regarding the underlying beliefs and perspectives that animate educational practice (Cranton 2006). Teachers continued to perceive themselves as learners no less than as experts in a particular field. Transformational learning theory scholar Patricia Cranton outlined a four-step process that made it possible to apply transformational theory in the preparation of adult educators, and then subsequently to their teaching. The four steps included "articulating assumptions"; "determining sources and consequences of assumptions"; "critical questioning"; and "imagining alternatives" (1996, 82–92). Referring to Mezirow, Cranton (1991) identified three kinds of reflection: *content*, *process*, and *premise* reflection. These modalities applied equally to the teacher and the learner. In particular, premise reflection was central to helping teachers develop a coherent philosophical basis for their teaching practice. Reflection, in this regard, related to investigating and analyzing the rationales that adult educators hold about teaching, and then assessing their validity in light of the their actual practice (Cranton 1996).

According to Cranton, teaching practice is grounded in content expertise on the one hand, and in the ability to critically reflect about the subject on the other hand. The process of assessing the assumptions about practice shared some relation to Donald Schoen's (1983; 1987) theory of the reflective practitioner. In his theory, however, the element of artistry in practice (called reflection-in-action) was as integral to the teacher's role as the subsequent analysis (called reflection-on-action); the latter descriptive construct bears a stronger resemblance to Cranton's application of critical reflection than the former.

Facilitation

Transformational learning theory researchers, however, also viewed the teacher as a facilitator. In contrast to theories of andragogy, where the primary responsibility of the teacher called for responding to the learners' articulated needs, here the teachers themselves explicitly modeled a thinking process so that the learners would become adept at critically evaluating their own experiences, beliefs, and knowledge. Through modeling, learners developed the capacity to reflect upon the assumptions and ideologies that underlay, informed, and guided their actions in the world (Brookfield 1989, 205). Brookfield's theories of facilitation and discussion (1985; 2005) and Mezirow's theories of discourse (2000) emphasized the ability of adult educators to model how to "take a critical stance . . . committed to questioning and exploring even the most widely accepted ideas and beliefs" (Brookfield 2005, 7).

Whether identified as central in andragogy or transformational learning theory, the facilitator identity of the teacher of adults can raise ethical questions for some scholars. In *Learning in Adulthood: A Comprehensive Guide,* Merriam and her colleagues noted that researchers rarely addressed issues regarding the extent and limits of an adult educator's moral responsibility in helping effect transformation in the attitudes, perspectives, and actions of adult learners (2007). They argued for further research on this subject in relation to the aims of transformational learning theory in particular. Similarly, Rossiter referred to investigations into teachers' responses to the "tension between stability and change in the learner's life" (1999, 58). Rossiter, summarizing scholar Carol Kasworm's ideas, wrote:

> As adult educators, we cannot help being involved in the psychosocial development of our learners. But, the question remains: Where is the line that separates challenging and helping learners achieve their own ends, from pushing learners into what we . . . consider to be growth and development? (Ibid.)

Such ethical issues are particularly vital for clergy to attend to, given their influence as moral exemplars in their congregations. I address them in the portraits and in the findings chapters.

Narrative Learning and the Role of the Teacher

With a few exceptions, narrative learning theories pay attention to the learners with less explicit attention to the adult educator. Much scholarship remains to be done in this area (Randall 1996; Rossiter and Clark 2007). Researchers still know very little about how adult educators conceptualize the value and purpose of narrative for themselves or their learners.

Although not driven by scholarly priorities, the Alban Institute has published a number of books and articles that attend to how stories shape congregational life and clergy leadership. To the extent that congregants and clergy live out their personal stories within a larger matrix of their communal and religious narratives, my research generates new insights regarding the central place of narrative in clergy educator identity and teaching practice. The rabbis in the following chapters discuss how stories from Jewish and non-Jewish sources shape their teaching. They relate the ways that their own personal narratives compel them to ask honest if difficult questions of themselves and their learners. They ponder the implications of the personal stories that their learners share with them.

Religious Education, Faith Development, Spirituality, and the Role of the Teacher

Three Christian scholars who have written about the intersection of religion, spirituality, and the practice of teaching authored valuable books in this broad area in the 1980s and 1990s. No study of teaching and religious education can ignore Maria Harris's contribution. In particular, her 1988 *Women and Teaching* examined metaphors of birth and midwifery that also emerged in my research as symbolically influential images for the rabbis in their teacher identity conceptions. Her classic 1987 *Teaching and Religious Imagination* proposed a way into contemplating religious education through the lens of aesthetics and artistic creativity. *Teaching from the Heart*, Mary Elizabeth Moore's 1998 book, invited readers to explore how theological processes, religious education, and educational theories dialogued with each other so as to generate holistic conceptions of teaching. While neither Harris nor Moore addressed teaching adults specifically, R.E.Y. Wickett's 1992 *Models of Adult Religious Education Practice* proposed practical approaches to reaching adult learners. Its comprehensiveness presented religious educators with an array of techniques for teaching adults.

Despite these valuable sources about teaching, there is much empirical research that awaits undertaking. How do adult educators distinguish between religion and spirituality in their teaching practice? Where do they derive their ideas about what adults need or desire from them as religious mentors or spiritual guides? To what extent does seminary teaching influence their educational interactions with adults? What models of excellence do seminary educators refer to in their own teaching about religious life, religious questions, faith, and spirituality? These questions need to be answered. The portraits of three outstanding rabbinic teachers of adults represent one such effort. The findings generated by them invite energetic dialogue and further research.

FROM ADULT EDUCATION TO ADULT JEWISH EDUCATION

Into this vast area of scholarship, the study of adult Jewish education dates only to the 1990s. The research has been generally empirical, relying upon qualitative methods such as interviews, focus groups, cases studies, and ethnography. Scholarship has integrated theories from adult education, psychology, sociology, and feminist studies. Adult development concepts, in particular those concerned with psychosocial, feminist, and narrative theories, entered into this research in significant ways. So, too, did transformational learning theory. Feminist theories that explored the relationship of gender, adult development, and adult education (Belenky et al. 1986; Hayes and Flannery 2000) substantively informed aspects of adult Jewish learning research. Diane Tickton Schuster's *Jewish Lives, Jewish Learning* (2003) and Lisa D. Grant et al.'s *A Journey of Heart and Mind: Transformative Jewish Learning in Adulthood* (2004) reflected the integration of these literature bases.

Schuster, a developmental psychologist by training, examined adult Jewish learning from the perspective of psychosocial developmental theories of adulthood. She also turned to feminist educational scholarship (2003). Grant et al. (2004) used transformational learning theory as a conceptual framework for investigating the dynamics of adult Jewish education. Schuster (1998; 1999; 2005), and Grant (2001; 2003; 2008) independently and together (2003; 2005; 2011) have pioneered the field. Research on teachers and teaching in adult Jewish education, however, is woefully absent (Woocher 2004; Schuster and Grant 2005; Grant and Schuster 2011). Schuster and Grant affirmed that despite anecdotal information, any widespread systematic research in this area lags far behind that of concentration on learners (2005). Two publications that straddled the boundary between practical guide and scholarly investigation point to this problematic gap. In 1990 Roberta Louis Goodman and Betsy Dolgin Katz, two leaders in the world of adult Jewish education practice, published *The Adult Jewish Education Handbook: Planning, Practice, and Theory*. As a practical guide to the field, it contained numerous essays and recommendations, but it did not advance the scholarly knowledge base. About two decades later, Betsy Dolgin Katz authored *Reinventing Adult Jewish Learning* (2012). For her book she spoke with graduates of the Florence Melton School of Adult Jewish Learning in order to understand the influence of this successful several-decade initiative in communal adult Jewish education. While the book offered valuable insights into the learners' experiences, it did not add new knowledge related to the adult Jewish educator.

From Scholar to Teacher

As a teacher I am often reminded of the benefits of educational theory. Exposure to it can widen the horizon of understanding of our beliefs, values, and practice. It does not, however, guarantee that we can or even want to apply it to our practice. Conversely, we may sincerely make every effort to do so, only to find the task harder than we envisioned. We may be unsettled when our expectations do not reach fruition. We may be delighted when an unanticipated outcome exceeds our hopes or offers us a different way of thinking about ourselves as teachers. I see familiarity with educational theory as a spur to examining practices, ideals, and aspirations. This book is an invitation for you to engage in such a process. The rabbis whose stories you will read about in the next chapters are known as outstanding teachers. Their excellence should not convey the impression that their maturity or skills have come easily and with little effort. If such were the case, it would hardly be necessary to devote an entire book to this subject. As a teacher of adults, I understand the level of attention, reflection, energy, and insight that was and is required to be the kind of teachers these rabbis are.

The Constellation of Narrative, Transformation, and Spirituality

Over the course of researching and writing this book, I inevitably reflected on my own teaching. The constellation of narrative, transformation, and spirituality spoke to me in unanticipated ways. These themes appear in the theoretical literature presented in this chapter. What they mean often varies, according to different authors, and with good reason: they rightly resist easy definition. More often than not they also function independently of one another as theoretical constructs. My research offers ways of conceptually integrating them, while presenting a rationale for doing so as well. The metaphor of a constellation invites adult educators to form their own understandings of how narrative, transformation, and spirituality affect their practice, rather than imposing my own preset definitions on them. The rabbis in the following chapters inspire me—and I hope you as well—to explore teacher identity and practice more fully through this constellation.

Indeed, when I turn to my teaching of adults, three memories that speak to this constellation stand out in particular.

My first experience as an adult educator took place more than a decade ago. For two years I was the educational director in a synagogue in Geneva, Switzerland. Although teaching a weekly course on the Torah was not initially part of my job description, I offered to do so. The rabbi, concerned because previous efforts in this regard failed, hesitantly agreed. As the only adult educator in the synagogue other than the rabbi, I was something of a novelty for the dozen learners who showed up at the first session. Most of them were old enough to be my grandparents. Represented were several Holocaust survivors, a few Sephardic transplants from North Africa, and one former Protestant pastor who had converted to Judaism many years earlier. I had heard some of their biographies in previous interactions but discovered more about them during our first class together. Needless to say, after this first meeting I wondered whether it was audacious of me to presume to teach them anything at all. They returned the following week. I had no choice but to keep going.

So it went for two years. Each week we delved into the Torah through a chronological journey that corresponded to the sacred calendar of readings that were chanted during worship. After a time I discovered that the many preconceptions they held in regard to the sacred text—it was either to be taken literally or to be dismissed as mythology, it would confirm or undermine their own beliefs about Jews and Judaism—began to peel away. The Torah surprised them. Its narratives upended their assumptions. Learning pushed them to explore their own religious attachments in new ways. Some of their discoveries unsettled their beliefs. Others allowed them to enter into their religious faith with new insights. Each week's text study seemed to organically lead us to discussions about these subjects.

Over the course of our time together, an issue that had been problematic for many of them—the historical accuracy of the Torah—lessened its hold. They began to see that while the Torah was not created as a history book in the modern sense, its truthfulness to their lives mattered a great deal more than they had anticipated it would. While these adult learners had always felt deeply tied to their Jewishness, through weekly study I witnessed the growth of new connections that struck me as profoundly spiritual. As their teacher I experienced a sense of awe and inspiration through participation in this transformation. That adults even in their sixth, seventh, and eighth decades of life were able to undergo such evolution *transformed me*. I went through a personal crisis of my own toward the end of our time together. One of the reasons I overcame it was thanks to the tremendous spiritual strength and hope I drew from these learners being in my life. In no small measure it was those two years with this group that set me on my present path.

A much more recent, and ongoing, teaching experience reminded me of how valuable it is to try new initiatives as an educator. In my current position as a professor of Jewish education, I teamed up with a rabbinic educator colleague to create a prayer program for our masters students. For two years we planned and designed what is now called the Liturgical Interpreters Project. That too many of our graduates left school without sufficient preparation in many areas of prayer was the early impetus driving this initiative. These gaps included lack of familiarity with the content of the liturgy, lack of confidence in leading worship, and lack of practice in teaching prayer. We also wondered about our students' own prayer lives. Many intriguing questions surfaced about this latter area as we designed the program.

Over the course of the two years of preparation, and even more strikingly during the first year of its launch in the fall of 2013, we realized the centrality of introspection and reflection to this process. As much as the young adult learners required knowledge about the liturgical content and performative religious ritual, they expressed a need to explore their emotions and beliefs toward prayer. As their facilitators, we deepened our mission from an emphasis on performance and pedagogy to a spiritual focus. We incorporated a spiritual journaling practice into the curriculum. This kind of writing developed into a forum through which the students could delve into their spiritual responses toward prayer in a reflective manner, either to be shared with the cohort or to be kept private.

Hearing our students' stories became another area for deep learning. A central touchstone of the program was the end-of-year meetings with the students. We met together with each one individually for an hour. At that time we invited them to give us their thoughts about their year of learning. We heard spiritual revelations, educational insights, and honest feedback during these three-way conversations. Many of them included stories of past prayer experiences in light of what they had undergone over the year. They told us about their memories of events during the year that triggered an assortment of ideas and feelings in them. We sifted through these together.

Our encounters pushed us, as their guides, to practice empathic listening. They motivated us to continue to experiment with new ways of holistically integrating spirituality, ritual, and performance into adult prayer education. Our Millenials responded in ways that excited and challenged us. As their mentors, we grew from teaching them. Rabbi Chanina's assertion in the Talmud, "I have learned much from my teachers, more from my colleagues, and the most from my students" (b. B. Ta'anit 7a) reverberated strongly as my colleague and I looked back and planned ahead for the second phase of the program.

My many years as a teacher affirm a message that the rabbis in this book reiterate again and again: To teach well means to keep learning. This learning surely includes content, but equally as vital is learning about oneself and one's learners. Just as a constellation is a collection of stars that form a visible pattern, this book invites you to imagine how the various patterns in your life form a whole, one that informs your sense of who you are as a religious educator. The endeavor extends well beyond the instrumental outcomes of any kind of teaching practice. It can become a portal into truths that await revelation. Through teaching and learning, adult religious educators discover the adventure of individual and collective transformation. We experience the multitude of ways in which education creates sacred space and transcendent purpose, thus filling up the wells of our spiritual selves. The Jewish sages Rabbi Chanina and Rabbi Shimon spoke about this kind of wisdom. In *Ethics of the Fathers* (m. 3–4) we read that Rabbi Chanina would say, " . . . if two sit together and the words of Torah [are spoken] between them, the Divine Presence rests between them . . . " A few lines later we read that Rabbi Shimon would say " . . . if three have eaten at one table and have spoken over it words of Torah, it is as if they have eaten from the table of the All-present, for it is written (Ezek 41:22) 'And he said to me, This is the table that is before the Eternal.'"

chapter 2

THE GARDENER

A discreet sign at the entrance to a long driveway off of a tree-lined suburban street is the sole indicator of the entrance to Sinai Temple. The original building that housed the synagogue, no longer in evidence, was a mansion on an expansive piece of secluded property. A small group of Jewish families who had been meeting regularly for several years purchased it when they founded the Reform congregation of Sinai Temple in 1948. In 2005 the synagogue completed a large construction project that added a brand new educational wing and renovated the main building.

Brightly illuminated hallways and a large foyer with cushioned benches impart a welcoming atmosphere. Both the exterior and the interior of the entire synagogue convey an immediate sense of light and airiness. Pamphlets on such topics as Torah, mitzvot, and spirituality sit at the front of the entrance. A plaque celebrates the recent success of the Education Building Fund. These seemingly inconsequential details suggest that education is a priority at Sinai Temple.

Approximately five hundred households belong to Sinai Temple. About half of the members live in the town, and the other half come from nearby suburban locales. According to an unofficial estimate by a former board member, approximately one third of the families include a spouse who is not Jewish. A rabbi, cantor, and rabbinic intern make up the clergy.[1] Several educational directors for programs ranging from nursery school to family education complete the professional staff. Since its founding, Sinai Temple has been led by only four rabbis. In 1997 the second rabbi retired, and the synagogue hired its first and only female rabbi. Although

---

1. The synagogue hired another full time rabbi in 2009.

highly regarded for her penetrating intellect, a rift developed between those who found her leadership style too scholarly and professorial, and those who supported her for these very same qualities. Rather than embroil the synagogue in a potentially divisive fight in order to preserve her post, she resigned before the end of her contract.

In 2003 the community engaged Jonathan Fisk. At the time of his hiring, Jonathan was in his mid-thirties and had held two positions elsewhere as an assistant rabbi. In addition to rabbinic ordination, Jonathan holds an MA in Jewish education. According to one synagogue leader, although Jonathan does not possess the same scholarly pedigree as his immediate predecessor, he is the right rabbi for the congregation. Congregants I spoke with frequently referred to Jonathan as a person who was approachable and easy to talk to, who remembers their names, who connects well with different age groups, and who reaches out to all congregants.

One of Jonathan's early accomplishments was the creation of a vision statement that articulates the six core values of the synagogue, expressed bilingually: Worship/*T'fillah*, Lifelong Learning/*Talmud Torah*, Community/*Kehillah*, Loving Kindness/*Hesed*, Repairing the World/*Tikkun Olam*, and Love of Israel/*Ahavat Israel*. These six values bear the strong imprint of Jonathan's own ideals. While the efforts to create this statement of values were a collaborative venture between laity and the rabbi, they reflect the influence of his presence as a religious leader and a rabbinic teacher. Jonathan views himself as a rabbi who helps his community generate visions of who they want to be. He guides them as they translate their ideals into practice. Such verbs as shaping, helping, and deriving figure prominently in Jonathan's description of his work as a rabbi. They point to an approach characterized by a collaborative effort between rabbi and congregants and by a constant movement back and forth between reflection and action.

MEETING JONATHAN

Jonathan saw our interviews as an opportunity for reflection. Furthermore, he found the timing fortuitous. Married, with three small children, he was a few months away from celebrating his fortieth birthday. He was also marking ten years in the rabbinate. He imagined the interviews as a way to consider his learning and his accomplishments over the past decade. Physically fit, of modest height, with dark brown hair and wire-rimmed glasses, dressed formally in a tie and suit, Jonathan exuded warmth with his firm handshake, direct eye contact, and broad smile. As I got to know Jonathan, I discovered that one of his strengths as a teacher of adults lies in his ability to balance a passionate commitment to Jewish tradition with personal warmth. These qualities form an equilibrium that makes him easy to approach as a rabbi. His sense of humor, including about the particularities of Judaism and the rabbinate, speaks to his ability to stand back from his experiences rather than being overwhelmed by the seriousness of his commitments.

Our three interviews took place in Jonathan's study.[2] It is a spacious, sunny room with a large desk, a computer, densely packed bookshelves, a sofa, two comfortable chairs, and a glass coffee table. Photographs of his children and of Israel abound. The study is on the second floor of the education wing, near the library, and set apart from the administrative center of the synagogue on the first floor. The location and decor speak to Jonathan's efforts to resist turning his rabbinate into an administrative or managerial position.

As the only rabbi at Sinai Temple at the time of my research, Jonathan spoke frankly about the tendency for a congregational rabbi to become a manager and a supervisor, rather than an educator. In one of our interviews he mentioned humorously but somewhat self-critically that it would be a good idea for him to put a sign above his desk, "You are a teacher of Torah." He admitted to needing to remind himself from time to time about why he chose the rabbinate.

A Varied Jewish Upbringing

When Jonathan was a child, Jewish community and Jewish ritual were integral to his family. They belonged to the local Conservative synagogue. Jonathan attended a secular Zionist summer sleepaway camp through eleventh grade. Both sides of his extended family were very involved in organized Jewish communal affairs. When it came time to send Jonathan and his sister to elementary school, his parents decided to enroll them in the local Orthodox Jewish day school. They did so less out of religious conviction than because several of Jonathan's close friends were attending the school. Its excellent academic reputation, as well as the fact that the children would receive a Jewish education during the week rather than on the weekend or

2. I interviewed Jonathan three times between March 8, 2008 and March 27, 2008. All further interview references refer to that time period.

after school, sealed the deal. Jonathan's enthusiastic engagement with Judaism surfaced early during his day school years. He especially found comfort and safety in Jewish learning.

This sense of warmth and connection helped him through the difficult time when as a seven-year-old his parents divorced. Each subsequently remarried, both to partners who were not Jewish. His mother married a secular man who, although he never converted, became a positive and influential person in Jonathan's evolving identity as a Jew. His father's second wife eventually converted to Judaism with a Reform rabbi. Although he was only one of two children of divorced parents in his class, in his school's loving environment he experienced a sense of stability as he traversed the family's reorganization.

After Jonathan graduated from day school in the eighth grade, there was no formal Jewish education at the Conservative synagogue to which his mother still belonged for him to join (the day school did not continue through high school). Jonathan's father proposed that he try studying with the Reform rabbi who had converted his stepmother. The rabbi was initiating a confirmation class for teenagers at his synagogue. Once again, Jonathan responded positively. It was this rabbi who shaped his adolescent positivity toward Judaism. He blended a profound care for his teenage students with a penetrating intelligence. Rather than lecture the teenagers, he framed his teaching as an invitation for the learners to grow personally. Jonathan described him as a role model because he put human beings rather than subject matter first. The ideal of a rabbi who helps people grow is central to Jonathan's conception of his rabbinic identity. It is a dominant motif in his teaching. It serves as a guiding image for his rabbinic calling.

However, after his confirmation at age fifteen and until his third year in college, Jonathan drifted away from formal Jewish education. When a cousin suggested that he accompany her for a semester in Israel, Jonathan agreed to go because he was not particularly happy at college. It turned out to be a transformative experience. He studied a wide range of courses related to Jewish themes. He discovered a renewed connection to Jewish learning and religious observance. In Israel he found a more mature relationship with God, religion, and community, one that he had not known as a teenager and young adult.

Upon his return from Israel he began integrating Judaism into his life more coherently. During his senior year he prayed with the Habad (a Hasidic movement) rabbi on campus, who happened to be a philosophy professor. He kept kosher. He became more fully involved in Jewish activities on campus. Yet he felt unsure about his future more generally.

Choosing the Rabbinate

Jonathan's stepfather visited him at college early in the spring semester of his senior year. At that time he suggested that Jonathan consider becoming a rabbi. He pointed out how much Jonathan loved Judaism, the Jewish people, Jewish learning, discussing Judaism, and even arguing about it. He cautioned Jonathan against choosing a career out of expediency or social pressure. For Jonathan it was a pivotal conversation. The proverbial "light bulb" moment happened. In the months following this talk, Jonathan immersed himself in research about rabbinical school and the rabbinate. He interviewed leaders of Jewish communal organizations who were not rabbis. He quickly realized that he wanted to incorporate spiritual and educational components in any work he undertook in the Jewish world. He spent the year after college studying, teaching, leading youth groups, and finding out if, in his words, he liked being "in the trenches of the synagogue" (he did), while figuring out where to apply to rabbinical school.

Given Jonathan's diverse experiences across a spectrum of Jewish movements and institutions, he did not feel wedded to any particular stream of Judaism. He realized that Hebrew Union College (HUC, the Reform Rabbinical Seminary) had a philosophy that was most similar to his own. He felt that its ideology of informed choice would give him the freedom to discover his commitment to Jewish observance and ritual at his own pace. Although he did not grow up as a Reform Jew, despite having studied with a Reform rabbi in high school, HUC helped him understand the seriousness of Reform Judaism. Another discovery he made during his years in seminary was that he learned best not through books but through people: by listening to them, by conversing with them, and by observing how they model behaviors that he admires. HUC provided him with multiple opportunities to learn in that way from peers and mentors. This orientation is central to his educational work with adult learners. The well-worn mantra, "I teach students not subjects," sounds accurate in Jonathan's case. Attentiveness to his learners comes before any preordained agenda he might have in mind for teaching them content.

JEWISH LEARNING AS A GARDEN

For Jonathan, Jewish life involves a dynamic process informed by two sources: people and Jewish tradition. Nineteenth-century European progressive educators, such as Johann Pestalozzi and Friedrich Froebel (the originator of the kindergarten), metaphorically compared teachers to gardeners, children to flowers, and education to gardens. Although their theories pertain to the education of children, the metaphors they invoke resonate with Jonathan's ideas about Jewish learning. To Jonathan, Jewish learning is the soil out of which a diversified garden—Jewish living—grows. The soil is rich and many layered. It has yielded abundantly for a very long time. It has been well tended, even during periods of drought or storm. The rabbi, as teacher, functions as the lead but far from the only gardener. The gardener is charged with being knowledgeable about the soil, the plants, the variety of trees and shrubs, and all the vegetation. The gardener also loves the garden and adores planting, cultivating, and sustaining it. He knows this garden well but is always delighted and intrigued by new growth. Sometimes he is perplexed or worried as well. He is aware that the garden is abundant and vulnerable. He is always looking for new ways to improve it and is passionate about introducing others to the joy involved in tilling the soil and making the garden bloom.

It may be that this metaphor presented itself to me during the course of one of my interviews with Jonathan. Not long before I met him, he had been on a synagogue trip to Israel, one of many that he has led for the congregation (and that he views as outstanding immersive communal opportunities for adult learning). This trip included a visit to a special Shabbat garden on a kibbutz. It was an outdoor, experiential-learning environment centered primarily on sensory elements of Shabbat. He spoke admiringly about the educational power of such a garden in a way that stoked my imagination. Illustrative of the garden metaphor to Jonathan's ideas about Jewish education is his procedure for preparing a couple for a wedding at which he will officiate. He shared with me the lengthy and involved educational process he undertakes with the couple. It includes meeting with them three or four times for a ninety-minute session to discuss their and his understandings of a Jewish wedding. He asks them to read Anita Diamant's *The New Jewish Wedding*. He gives them three pages with questions about marriage to which they write individual responses; this is followed by time spent together with him going over their responses. Finally, he invites them to write their own personal *ketubah* (Jewish wedding contract), which they then share with him.

The process highlights how Jonathan creates an environment in which Jewish learning is intended to connect to a person's whole life. Adult learning is an activity that integrates thinking, feeling, creating, and doing. When sustained, it leads to personal transformation. Jonathan spoke definitively about his view that every interaction with a congregant is an "opportunity for learning, for growth, and for connection . . . for teaching." It is true that Jonathan is alert to the possibility that any encounter with a congregant might offer him the chance to teach. He also recognizes that his ideal does not always translate into reality. There are times when it is also unnecessary. As a result, he has come to the conclusion that giving special attention to those settings where teaching and learning reflect intentionality is the necessity. It is the environments where Jonathan carefully plans and reflects upon the learning and motivates the adults to be active participants with him that qualify for him as truly educational. While he cites retreats, trips, and camp as his favorite opportunities for teaching because the learners can make immediate connections between something Jewish and what is happening to them in the moment, Jonathan spends more time from week to week in more conventional formal settings.

JONATHAN'S COURSES

At the time of my research Jonathan taught four ongoing courses for adults. These included the following:

- An hour-long Shabbat morning weekly Torah discussion and study in the main sanctuary that follows a shortened Shabbat morning service for the entire congregation and often precedes a Bar or Bat Mitzvah that is attended primarily by friends and family of the child. The Torah study group existed before Jonathan's arrival; the idea for it was initiated by one of its current members, who is one of the synagogue's founders. It is composed of a core group of twenty-five to thirty regulars, many of whom have been participating in it for years. The age range is primarily from people in their fifties to eighties, with the older participants more numerous than the younger ones. There is a fairly even distribution between men and women in this group.

- A biweekly, seminar-style Torah study discussion and study group that meets in the social hall during the week in the morning for an hour and a half. Jonathan created the class after arriving at Temple Sinai. He leads the group through various books of the Bible that are chosen in a collaborative fashion. The class takes place around several large tables, similar to a college seminar. The participants engage in close reading and analysis of Torah texts, studying them from various perspectives ranging from the historical, to the theological, to the personal. Approximately twenty-five to thirty learners attend this group, with a larger representation of learners in their sixties and above, with women outnumbering men most of the time.
- A once-a-month, seven AM weekly Torah study created by Jonathan to encourage congregants whose work schedules make it difficult for them to come to his other courses because of time constraints to study with him. Approximately a dozen adults attend regularly, mostly men who work full-time jobs.
- A bimonthly adult Bar and Bat Mitzvah class that meets in the library, to which Jonathan has given a Hebrew name: *Anshei Bina*. Congregants who seek to increase their basic knowledge of Judaism attend. It is a two-year course that Jonathan co-teaches with a rabbinic intern. Jonathan teaches history, theology, prayer, and life-cycle events. The intern teaches Hebrew language and Hebrew liturgy. Jonathan deliberately calls this course *Anshei Bina*, which translates into English roughly as "People of Wisdom" rather than "Adult Bar and Bat Mitzvah." Jonathan remarked that rather than calling the class, "Adult Bar and Bat Mitzvah," he consciously sought a name that was egalitarian and reflected what he believes many adults yearn for—*binah*—or understanding and meaning.

In the first three classes, a noticeable overlap exists among the adult learners who attend. There is a core group of devoted adult learners of approximately twenty to twenty-five people who study regularly with Jonathan and in the other ongoing adult educational courses offered at the synagogue. Another thirty attend more or less regularly. Finally, there is the remaining adult membership who comes sporadically to thematic programs or scholar-in-residence weekends.

The Gardener

Themes in Jonathan's Teaching

Teaching, Not Preaching

As recorded in the biblical book of Exodus, chapter 31, Betzalel is the character who designed a portable sanctuary for God during the Israelites' wanderings. He is one of Jonathan's favorite biblical personalities. While Betzalel is typically known as an artist, to Jonathan he is above all a teacher. He took his wisdom, understanding, and knowledge and used them, in Jonathan's words, "to empower" the people to bring God's presence among them. Betzalel helps his fellow Israelites build the Tabernacle as a beautiful structure. In so doing he teaches them how to create a holy space in their midst.

Jonathan's interpretation of Betzalel's role as a teacher encapsulates an explicit idea at the center of his conception of teaching: He distinguishes between teaching and preaching. In the former, he strives to open up a dialogue through study as a way of motivating people to consider what Judaism means to their everyday lives. This process contrasts with a preaching style that involves exhorting his learners how to live without engaging them in an exchange of perspectives. In this vein Jonathan recalled an important encounter when he was a rabbinical student intern that pushed him to think about what he hoped to accomplish as a rabbinic educator. He was teaching Hebrew and liturgy to a group of adults preparing for their adult Bar and Bat Mitzvah ceremony when a learner challenged him about his explanation as to why the first and last Hebrew letters of the *Sh'ma* prayer (whose words appear originally in Deut 6:4) appear enlarged in a Torah scroll and often in the prayer book. The traditional explanation is that they form the Hebrew word "witness." Rabbinic tradition uses this peculiar font alteration to explain that Jews are witnesses to the monotheistic ethos. The learner was dissatisfied with this explanation and spoke up. Her questioning of a hallowed premise helped Jonathan realize that such active interaction was to be welcomed and supported, even when it contradicted the accepted wisdom of tradition.

Along with inviting challenges to received wisdom from his adult learners, Jonathan also refrains from judgmental responses to their ideas. The two dimensions of this approach to his learners are part of what he intends by differentiating teaching from preaching. In our interviews Jonathan cited several reasons why he believes that the focus on "teaching, not preaching" needs to guide his educational work with adults. Among the most prominent of these are the ideological orientation of the Reform movement (one that encourages informed choice about religious practice), the educational level of most of his adult congregants (college and beyond), and his relative youthfulness (years in the rabbinate and age of his congregants). Each of these affects how Jonathan conceptualizes his role as a teacher of adults.

Influence Instead of Authority

In Jonathan's experience, Reform rabbis have a fair amount of influence but little authority over their congregants in matters of religious practice and belief. As a Reform rabbi, he likes that he has more flexibility in interpreting Jewish tradition than rabbis who represent the traditional movements. Whereas Orthodox Judaism will give people clear answers in a world that can seem confusing or purposeless, Reform rabbis use education as a guide. They value an individual's autonomy. While he sees limits to this approach on some matters, such as circumcision, it is one that Jonathan embraces. As a Reform rabbi, Jonathan also does not seek to tell learners how they should respond to Jewish tradition and to Jewish rituals or religious law. Even if he were to do so, such an approach would in all likelihood meet resistance because of the kinds of adults he encounters in his congregation. Early experiences in several congregations helped him arrive at this understanding.

Well-Educated Learners

Jonathan emphasized that the majority of adult members at Sinai Temple are predominantly college-educated, high-achieving professionals. Many are erudite about a range of fields related to their careers or to personal interests. Educational attainments and life experiences inevitably influence their attitudes toward Jewish learning. Despite his rabbinic title and the learning that stands behind it, Jonathan believes that dictating how adults should live their lives in the context of Judaism would be met with challenge, and perhaps even hostility. He summed up the anticipated response of congregants by the question, "Well, who are you to tell me?" Although Jonathan cites occasions when he finds that as a rabbi he has had to say, "This is how you should proceed," more often he sees his role as teacher to be that of a catalyst for reflection.

The Gardener

One of the regulars who attends the Shabbat morning study group weekly told me that when Jonathan first arrived at the synagogue, he was more inclined to use Torah study as an opportunity to give mini-sermons. The learners felt that he did not provide time for dialogue and they told him so. He listened to their feedback, adjusted his approach, and worked to develop his discussion facilitation skills. The learner saw this transition as a reflection of Jonathan's ability as a rabbinic teacher. Rather than imposing a preconceived notion of what mattered on his learners, he chose to examine his own teaching practice to better align it with the needs of his congregants.

Jonathan underscored that as members of a democratic society, the hierarchical rabbinic prerogative of earlier eras no longer applies to rabbis of his generation or his kind of Jewish community. Instead, his charge revolves around motivating adults to study so that they will feel empowered. They will come to understand more about how Jewish tradition can affect every aspect of their lives. He hopes that in so doing they will take further steps to act on their new insights. Action involves potential changes in their personal choices around a host of matters, from social justice to ritual observance. It also includes participation in Jewish communal life as an expression of their evolving identity as Jewish adults.

Stories as Bridges

While Jonathan pays careful attention to the difference between teaching and preaching in his rabbinate, he frequently uses stories to bridge the two. He makes use of Jewish and universal stories, as well as ones from his personal life. Jonathan mentioned that one of the benefits of stories is that they "paint pictures" (in his words), using images and metaphors that often illuminate a value-driven message. As a result people may be able to engage with values-laden ideas more willingly than they would be in a sermon that lacks any narrative element. This is not to say that he is trying to preach a message surreptitiously through a story. Rather, stories enable adults to see their own existential circumstances reflected and refracted through the lens of the narrative. As a result, stories promote critical reflection. They still give Jonathan an opportunity to transmit essential values he finds significant, but without moralizing. In this way, he incorporates into his teaching some of the style of the pre–World War Two Eastern European *magid*, or itinerant preacher, for whom stories formed an essential part of his repertoire.[3]

However, at certain times of the year, such as during the High Holidays, congregants expect that the rabbi will preach. Here, too, Jonathan uses stories. He incorporates storytelling as a teaching strategy within his sermons. In this context its purpose and outcome are different than in smaller settings when the adults come specifically to study. With a large audience of worshipers, storytelling aims to create a connection between the rabbi and the attendees at a moment of high intensity in the Jewish calendar. Through personal stories about his own life that are interspersed into a sermon, Jonathan can speak from an "I" place. He tries to bridge the inevitable distance that exists between the clergy and the laity at a time when large numbers of people congregate together and a sense of intimate closeness all but vanishes.

As an example, he shared with me that his sister had died a few years earlier. He had felt a need to talk about her death with the community at the *yizkor* (memorial) service during Yom Kippur. But he wanted to tell his story in the context of "what happens after we die and where we go." These are themes naturally linked to the liturgy of the Jewish New Year and Penitential season. He found a story about the afterlife that was not from a Jewish source. In his sermon at the memorial service he shared it. It raised core issues that he knew from pastoral encounters congregants struggle with, more often than not on their own: What happens to our loved ones after they die? If they could come back and tell us, would we recognize them if we saw them? Would we believe them? What will happen to me when I die?

His choice reflected an effort to integrate, via the narrative of his sister's death and the story he found, the *yizkor* ritual and the many profound questions that the High Holidays may trigger. Given his own grieving about his sister's death, he chose not to suppress or hide his thoughts about mortality. During the sermon he spontaneously wept in front of the congregation. Far from unsettling the congregants, his openness moved many of them to speak to him afterward. In this way, even when he delivers sermons, Jonathan blends personal stories and others he has read or heard to reach out to congregants. By so doing he hopes to familiarize congregants with their rabbi as a human being who struggles in ways similar to them.

---

3. For further reading on the place of the *magid* in Eastern European Jewish communities, see http://www.yivoencyclopedia.org/article.aspx/Talk/Professional_Talkers.

He invites them to begin a dialogue with him about potentially charged subjects.

Rabbi as Co-Learner

Reform Judaism established the precedent of a pulpit rabbi whose essential function was to deliver weekly sermons to a congregation. Jonathan's emphasis on teaching as distinct from preaching offers a different model. Yet neither does Jonathan present himself as a rabbinic scholar who is light years ahead of his adult learners in Jewish knowledge and wisdom. Although his Jewish learning is extensive, as a teacher he imagines himself very much as a co-learner when in the company of adults. Accordingly, teacher and learner interact on a more egalitarian basis. Jewish learning becomes part of a collaborative process. It is intended to help adults view their experiences, Jewish and general, from new perspectives. They become a group of individuals who coalesce around a project that dedicates them to searching for new understandings. The rabbi acts as an expert partner rather than an expert lecturer or preacher.

The term "seeing" came up frequently in our interviews. Seeing was an image for Jonathan that underscored the importance to him of insight, or in its closest Hebrew translation, *binah*. Teaching and learning are activities that enable adults to stand back and view their lives in new or more nuanced ways. Jewish education, when successful, enriches, transforms, and generates insight. Teaching for this kind of understanding means bringing adult learners into an ancient conversation that is up to them to renew. Learning draws them out of themselves and their customary ways of interpreting their lives. Yet a rabbi must never use coercion or pressure as a way of getting adults to follow a particular path, even when there is one favored by the rabbinic educator.

Finding Personal Relevance in Torah

Jonathan defines Torah broadly as "Jewish wisdom and Jewish knowledge." More specifically it is, "anything that has been written or passed or retold that was intended to be Jewish in its teaching." Jonathan believes that Jewish learning helps lead adults to explore Judaism's power to shape all areas of a person's life. The process might include decisions as different as the kind of coffee to buy and how to conduct oneself sexually in a relationship.

He hopes that his adult learners will discover in Judaism a level of comfort, safety, sustenance, and coherence that he has found in it. This reality applies even when the learning challenges them to absorb new information or new perspectives. It is what Jonathan means by the phrase "personal relevance."

From personal experience Jonathan recognizes that his approach sometimes can be disruptive on any number of levels. During the course of his rabbinic studies, he struggled mightily for a while with theological issues. In particular, the idea of the Bible as a humanly created and constructed document pushed him to evaluate most of the messages he had been taught as a child about the origins of the Torah. Inevitably, and in particular when they begin to study regularly, the adults he teaches face issues that put them in confrontation with cherished or accepted beliefs. Jonathan seeks to guide them so that the outcome of such confrontation is a new or renewed sense of Judaism, rather than a rejection of it or the new knowledge sparked by learning. He does not want learners to feel alienated. He does, however, acknowledge that his teaching philosophy contains such a risk. Helping learners find personal relevance as a way to integrate what they learn constructively into their lives represents both a strategy and an aim of his teaching.

Teaching Strategies

The task of guiding his learners toward personal relevance in relation to Judaism requires invoking various teaching strategies. Five strategies guide Jonathan: asking open-ended questions; listening to the learners' perspectives and experiences without judgment; encouraging discussion among the learners; distinguishing between existential or spiritual truths and historical facts; and referring to contemporary concerns and issues for comparison and contrast. Jonathan draws on these techniques as he and his learners tackle why being a Jew matters to them, and why Judaism means much more than ethnic nostalgia. They jointly investigate a wide array of topics, as varied as God, ritual, prayer, community, ethics, spirituality, history, identity, politics, and the natural environment, most often with a biblical text as the source.

For example, in his bimonthly Bible study class, the textual content often becomes a gateway to explore a crucial and often suppressed question for the adults he teaches: "When do people actively seek spirituality?" While the learners study various biblical passages, Jonathan returns to this broad question from the perspective not only of the Bible's narratives, but also from that of his participants. He invites them to reflect on the importance of age, class, and life-cycle transitions in their own lives in relation to the text.

Even with the array of strategies that Jonathan demonstrates during his courses, he admits that achieving such personal relevance can be elusive for many adults. The process is a highly individual one. Each adult learner brings a complex life history to the learning, as well as a welter of attitudes and feelings about Judaism. That history and those feelings affect each and every one of them. The search is pursued in a group setting, which means that there are as many life histories as there are people in the room. How can the teacher keep in mind so many individuals?

Those learners who study regularly are more likely to benefit from Jonathan's emphasis on personal relevance than those who participate sporadically. It becomes an ever-present refrain in Jonathan's approach and a referential theme in the adults' reflections. The learners begin to appreciate that connecting their whole lives to Jewish learning is at the heart of studying as a Jew. A regular commitment enhances this possibility. Some, as a result, may avoid it for just this reason. In our interviews, Jonathan referred to numerous instances when he and his learners struggle constantly around key issues. As their teacher it helps that he knows many of his learners' backgrounds because he is their congregational rabbi. He has established relationships with most of them over an extended period of time and in other synagogue settings and interactions. It is one reason why being with them as part of his overall rabbinic duties enriches his teaching.

Jonathan does not shy away from sharing with his learners the reality that he and other rabbis he knows wrestle with the tradition's relevance to their lives no less than lay Jews. He related a particularly memorable conversation with a congregant that took place immediately prior to one of our interviews:

> I had lunch with a fellow from the synagogue. He had invited me out for lunch and he said, "You know, I'm here because I was raised Jewish. We live in a community right now where there are lots of Jewish families. And I'm not sure why it's important to be Jewish. Can't I just be a good person?" He wanted a conversation. He started out by saying, "One of the biggest problems is that I don't believe in God." To which I always ask, "Tell me what is it about God that you don't believe?" And he described the omniscient, omnipresent, omnipotent God. And I said, "That's great. I don't

believe in that God either." But for him it was, "Well, wait, you're a rabbi, and you don't believe in this kind of God? You say these prayers and this doesn't work for you?"

Then I wrote him an e-mail this morning and I said, "I realize that if you say you don't believe in God, the only other options are, 'Then what could you believe in, and what else could it look like?' But for most of us ... when we say, 'Well, if we're going to reject this, then we reject it; therefore, if I don't believe in God, then God isn't or can't be part of my life,' as opposed to reframing and redesigning it. When you give up on that concept of God ... you then have to step back and come up with a different image, perhaps that may not be as dramatic but is no less satisfying ... " I said, "That's a step in developing your God concept." That was part one. And the other thing I said to him was, "This is just my theory."

Jonathan's teaching of adults includes informal one-on-one mentoring of congregants that develops as part of learning. Sometimes these one-on-one sessions lead to participation in a group. Mentoring may play a greater part in Jonathan's teaching than even he recognizes. The better he knows his congregants, the more he may be able to shape his teaching with an awareness of their stories, concerns, and dilemmas in mind. All of the adult learners I spoke to referred positively to Jonathan's interpersonal skills. His strength in this area suggests that the one-on-one relationships he develops with congregants affect his teaching positively. Creating further such mentoring opportunities would be an additional way to facilitate the development of personal relevance among adult congregants. The approach would be especially helpful for those who do not feel as if they have found their place yet in the synagogue. It may also benefit members who have questions that cannot be adequately addressed in a group setting. On a practical note, for congregants whose schedules make it difficult to attend regular classes, individualized mentoring provides the possibility for greater flexibility. Would Jonathan be willing to set aside time in his busy day for more of these kinds of exchanges on a regular basis? How much additional effort would be required to expand his teaching repertoire to build this sort of mentoring into it intentionally?

TEACHING FROM THE HEART

For Jonathan adult Jewish education involves responding with the heart. It opens the possibility for being vulnerable in the presence of others by

The Gardener

both the rabbi and the learners. Not all adults are ready to place themselves voluntarily in such a position unless they feel secure that their teacher is a trustworthy person. They may require a more personal relationship with the rabbi before launching into a group environment. It is true that the personal disclosure that often occurs in Jonathan's classes establishes close relationships among the learners and with the rabbi. Learning creates and fortifies emotional and social bonds. Interpersonal connections motivate these learners to attend week after week. A sense of belonging, albeit without being exclusionary, characterizes the gatherings where Jonathan teaches. Even secular moments, such as birthdays and retirements, are recognized as part of the back and forth in Jonathan's study groups. Learning contributes to bonds of warmth and intimacy. Coming together from week to week creates a sense of attachment and belonging among the learners and toward Jonathan. An adult who wants these kinds of connections will flourish. Those who may not are likely to feel less inclined to make any kind of ongoing commitment.

There is no simple resolution to this question of adult learner preference. Adult learning is an entirely voluntary choice, driven by factors that range from the mundane (habit), to the complex (a personal crisis). A rabbi's style can attract or repel an adult. Not every adult congregant will find Jonathan's emphasis on personal relevance appealing. Jonathan is aware of this reality. However, because he has reflected carefully on the meaning and aims of adult learning, his teaching comes from a place of authenticity. He is honest about what he believes to be of value, and he shows respect for his adult congregants by standing by his ideals. He may lose or fail to attract some adults. But it also means that they can trust that their rabbi is honest with them. He does not have a covert agenda to promote.

Asking Open-Ended Questions

This openness about his educational values is an essential element to Jonathan's success with adults. Many of his adult congregants view Jewish tradition as paradoxically comforting and perplexing simultaneously. The experience of the group helps them meet the challenges that some of the content of Jewish tradition poses spiritually, intellectually, and emotionally. Asking open-ended questions about sacred texts and topics stands out as a central way that Jonathan helps the group mediate the tension that this paradox generates.

Jonathan believes that a willingness to ask questions is rooted in traditional talmudic approaches to Jewish learning. His conviction influences the importance he ascribes to questioning. Open-ended questions—in other words, ones that do not have obviously right or wrong, true or false answers—act as powerful prompts for adults to approach a subject from their unique perspectives. Jonathan will ask such questions as, *What else does this text evoke for you? Are there other situations in your life where you can relate to this text? Where this makes sense?*

I observed, for example, a session on the subject of Shabbat in the adult Bar and Bat Mitzvah class in which Jonathan asked about the idea of Sunday as the American Shabbat. He did this by way of comparison and contrast with the Jewish version. Several women who had previously been silent became very animated. One mentioned that in Boston, where she grew up, the stores were all closed on Sunday when she was a child. Another recalled that during her childhood, the city she lived in was quiet on Sunday because there was very little business activity. Jonathan's open-ended query triggered obvious involvement in the topic. The learners began to contextualize the subject through their own experiences even though the memories were not specifically Jewish in nature.

Part of Jonathan's emphasis on open-ended questions derives from his commitment to posing these kinds of questions to himself: *What am I doing? Why am I choosing a particular path or decision? What might I need to change in myself as I evolve as a person, husband, father, son, Jew, and rabbi?* To ask is a basic mode through which he relates to himself, to his world, and to other people. His teaching style reflects this stance. In addition, as a Reform rabbi he places the emphasis on asking questions rather than giving answers. He believes that adults can and must decide for themselves how to relate Jewish tradition to their lives.

The use of open-ended, broad questions invites learners to participate actively rather than passively in decisions about leading a Jewish-infused life. This is an outcome that Jonathan perceives as one of the aims of his teaching. His confidence in his adult learners' ability to find their own answers often challenges them. He wants them to push themselves, albeit gently, to establish connections between Jewish learning and their lives. He does not believe in Jewish authority figures, such as rabbis, delivering prefabricated answers. As a consequence, his teaching style involves modeling for his learners a deepening sense of personal accountability and responsibility in shaping a Jewish life. On the one hand, each learner needs to make his or her own choices about what to do with his or her learning. On the other hand, learning together creates a sense of a participatory journey, where each learner's perspective and experiences, including the rabbi's, contributes to an accumulated wisdom bank within the community.

Adult Development Matters

Throughout our interviews, Jonathan returned frequently to his awareness that adult learners' developmental needs are different than those of children and adolescents. These needs must be addressed, respected, and valued in order for learning to flourish. Certain episodes or triggers in adults' lives affect their openness to learning. Furthermore, familiarity with his adult learners' backgrounds plays a part in how Jonathan approaches a subject in order to elicit meaningful engagement. Jonathan generally knows a reasonable amount about his learners' careers, hobbies, and families. He discovers their level of Jewish learning, religious background, and religious conflicts. This privileged knowledge provides him with insights into how they might respond to a particular subject or text.

In our interviews Jonathan pointed out several significant differences that he has observed between adult learners and children, noting especially the following:

- Adults, because of their life experience, bring different skills to the learning environment in comparison to children and teenagers, who spend most of their time in compulsory school environments.
- Jewish adults are highly sensitive to how much they do not know about Jewish subjects.
- Adults carry a trove of memories and experiences to their learning, both Jewish and general.
- Adults need opportunities to teach as well as to learn, as part of gaining confidence and increasing their commitment to Jewish learning.
- Adults tend to struggle with the difference between historical truth and existential truth in relation to the biblical texts.

As their teacher Jonathan attends to these differences. When he falters in this regard, as sometimes has happened, he believes that the learning often falls flat. It fails to reach the learner in any substantive manner. He is particularly sensitive to the feelings of shame among many of his novice adult learners that they should know more about Judaism. Such shame can deter them from pursuing Jewish learning. To counter this emotion, he pays close attention to validating what they do know and valuing the perspectives they bring. He also is sensitive to how his tone of voice or choice of words might unintentionally give the impression that he is condescending to them. Adult learning is an entirely voluntary effort for his congregants. As their teacher, he wants to visibly honor that choice. Body language, choice of words, and tone of voice all affect how his learners respond to him, and, by extension, to learning.

He also realizes that the decision to study Jewish subjects with a rabbi in a group can be (and often is) initially an anxiety-producing step. He finds that adults bring many questions and assumptions about Jewish tradition, religion, and God to their learning. These often emerge over time when the adult learner feels safe enough to expose them. Precisely because of this reality, Jonathan wants to affirm their knowledge, experiences, and memories and incorporate them into the learning process. Doing so helps the learners establish connections between their lives and Jewish learning, the vital outcome that Jonathan seeks for them. The result of learning is much more than an increased knowledge base for the learner. Crucially, it potentially transforms the learners' perspectives about themselves in relation to Judaism. Study becomes a pathway to furthering personal development.

Jonathan sets his goals very high. In spite of his keen awareness and his sensitivity, he can overlook his own insights about the particular learning needs of adults. This occurs most often when he has a curriculum that he feels he needs to complete, such as for the two-year adult Bar and Bat Mitzvah class that I observed. In this instance, Jonathan seemed preoccupied with transmitting information. These classes contrasted strongly with many of the other settings. In the latter ones a biblical text and the themes it elicited, rather than a particular topic, generated discussion. It may be, however, that the learners in the Bar and Bat Mitzvah class seek the kind of factual knowledge that Jonathan conveys efficiently through a more frontal teaching approach.

Situations when learners may require a more frontal style, and when transmission of basic information is asked for as part of the learning process, should not be neglected as a legitimate way of teaching adults. In this regard, Jonathan may be instinctively responding to his adult learners by shifting how he teaches. The issue to explore in this instance is whether, in

The Gardener

line with his articulated values of creating a more democratic atmosphere, Jonathan does enough to find out what his learners want and need in such a context.

Adult Development and Text Study

Sacred texts constitute the primary subject matter in Jonathan's work with adults. The Bible is his most regular source. He has discovered that once adults get comfortable with text study, they become impressively enthusiastic. However, to succeed they must study the texts in English translation. Language can alienate or include. Indeed, Jonathan undoubtedly empathizes with his learners on this subject. He shared with me that foreign-language acquisition is difficult for him. He continues to work at thoroughly mastering spoken Hebrew. Jonathan emphasized that given the choice to do close analysis of a Jewish text in English or to be lectured about it by him, the adults respond with a very high level of engagement to the former. Jonathan likes to coax his adult learners toward a sense of mastery of text study. While Hebrew is the sacred tongue, English is the way in to the depths of Judaism's sources for his learners.

In turn, once his learners develop confidence in their capabilities it gives Jonathan the opening to guide them to develop a new skill set: he wants them to view themselves as teachers of Torah. To see that they are capable of leading discussions with their peers (even sometimes in the presence of their rabbi) increases their positivity toward the texts and Jewish learning more generally. It stimulates their commitment to come back for more. By initiating such participation, Jonathan mentors the learners to become lay teachers. He helps create a learning environment in the synagogue that is inclusive rather than elitist.

A final matter regarding text study that Jonathan raised in the interviews and that surfaced in my observations of his classes concerns the issue of historical truth in the biblical narratives. Jonathan distinguishes history from philosophical, existential, spiritual, and religious concerns that transcend particular historical epochs. The majority of Jonathan's text-based teaching involves the Bible. He finds that many of his adult learners can become focused on the historical validity or context of a source. But he believes that this angle is not the one that ultimately benefits his learners. Yes, it can be tantalizing to examine the archaeological discoveries and see whether they corroborate or undermine the Bible. Although Jonathan acknowledges their interest and even shares it some of the time, he wants to broaden the way his adult learners understand the richness of these sacred sources. This stance ties in with his emphasis on adult development and finding personal relevance in Torah. In Jonathan's own words: "People like to know the historical context. That how we're taught, that's how we're raised—'Is it true? Is it not true? Did it really happen?' And I always say, 'Does it matter?' Or they'll say, 'Is this true?' And I'll say, 'Are you asking me is it true, or are you asking me did it happen?' Two different questions."

Jonathan's distinction between historical events and existential truths that transcend particular historical epochs represents an attempt to move adults away from a perspective on Torah study that they often bring from their childhood. As children, his adult learners were taught to think of the Bible's stories as historically accurate. But in the course of their secular education they discovered discrepancies between the message they assimilated as Jewish learners and new knowledge gained about ancient history and science. As a result, when they return to the Bible as adults they sometimes receive it through the teaching they absorbed as children. This developmental disconnect can prevent them from approaching sacred texts in new ways that will help them generate adult connections.

Jonathan knows that letting go of assumptions that are deeply rooted in childhood, and replacing them with a more complex view of the Bible in particular may initially disrupt his learners' beliefs. Jonathan relishes that part of his role as a rabbinic teacher involves facilitating that perspective transformation. He knows that it often requires a change in the learner's relationship to Judaism. As their teacher, he is there to support and guide them as they transition to a new kind of understanding of Judaism via text study. But it is precisely during that journey when he witnesses the most growth.

A WELL-TENDED GARDEN

In 2008 the influential British educator Sir Ken Robinson delivered one of his many TED talks.[4] In it Robinson described teachers as gardeners. He referred to the life cycle of a human being as including both "seasons of personal growth and development and seasons that are fallow." The purpose of a teacher, like that of a gardener or farmer, according to Robinson, is to "know what the conditions of growth are" so that the learners flourish.

---

4 https://www.youtube.com/watch?v=rql7SFey5Mo.

He underscored that such teaching applies not to young people alone but should be accessible throughout our lives.

Jonathan's teacher identity as a rabbi speaks to Robinson's description. To Jonathan, our backgrounds, memories, and experiences form the rich soil within which adult learning germinates. Rabbis need to value the ground out of which their learners emerge, even as they till new soil together. As a teacher of adults, Jonathan the gardener demonstrates that rabbinic educators continue to sustain a tradition when they cultivate it alongside their learners as partners in a transformative endeavor. Dedication to that activity enriches both the people who engage in it and the tradition of which it is a part.

A particularly memorable Shabbat morning occurred during the months I visited Sinai Temple. I joined the Shabbat Torah study and listened as Jonathan and his learners discussed the portion that begins the cycle of Jacob narratives in Genesis. Some of the participants expressed vocal dismay at the critical tone they heard embedded in the text directed towards Jacob's sons' unethical behavior. In the course of the conversation Jonathan introduced a bit of tension-breaking levity when he mentioned, "We come from a line of crooks and criminals." But before ending the session he gently reminded the group that Jacob's sons were "still evolving people. They're unfinished." His comment reflects a guiding principle toward which he aspires as a rabbinic teacher: No less than the characters in the biblical narrative, both he and his adult learners are growing human beings. Learning offers us the hope and the promise of renewal and transformation as we move through the seasons of our lives.

chapter 3

THE MIDWIFE

At Temple Agudath Or, a Reform synagogue with a membership of approximately six hundred fifty families, Rabbi Rina Lewin is one of two rabbis who share rabbinic responsibilities.[1] Agudath Or, founded in 1923, is located in an ethnically and racially diverse suburb with a substantial and stable Jewish population. It is also within close walking distance of the city's Conservative, Orthodox, and Reconstructionist synagogues. Jewish life in this area has flourished in the twentieth century. To the first-time visitor at Agudath Or, the sprawling and well-maintained complex conveys the impression of a secure institution. During Rina's tenure it has transformed itself from a classic Reform synagogue of the first half of the twentieth century into one that seeks to respond to a new generation of twenty-first-century American Jews. It also embodies some of the shifting ideas in the Reform movement. Prominent among these is an enthusiastic embrace of more Hebrew in the liturgy and an exploratory openness to traditional ritual practices.

MEETING RINA

Known nationally as an outstanding rabbinic teacher and religious leader in the American Jewish community, Rina first came to my attention through articles in the Jewish press. Locally, her name came up frequently as one of the best teachers of adults in the area. Although interested in the project, she expressed concern about the time commitment given her full schedule.

1. Agudath Or, a Hebrew pseudonym, in English translates as "Congregation of Light."

The Midwife

She wanted to meet me face to face before deciding to go forward. During the many months I spent in Rina's company, I discovered how much interpersonal connections reside at the heart of her rabbinic identity and her practice as a teacher of adults.

At our first encounter I met a pale, tall, slim woman in her mid-fifties with the graceful posture of a dancer. But she wore a pantsuit that seemed deliberately to lend more than a touch of the professional executive to her presence. Rina struck me initially as personally reserved but genuinely interested in my project. Entering her spacious office I noticed photographs of what I presumed were her family jockeying for space on her desk and on the walls with paintings by children from the synagogue's religious school. A large window looked out onto a playground. Toddlers' voices buoyantly wafted from it through the air into her office. Family, children, and community were words that immediately came to mind as I settled into my seat. A collection of posters spoke to an awareness of women's issues. A prominent one from the Religious Coalition for Reproductive Choice rested on an easel at the entrance to the office bearing the slogan "Pro-Faith, Pro-Family, Pro-Choice." Although Rina rarely referred to gender issues during our interviews, my subsequent observations of her teaching and my informal interviews with many of her learners suggest strongly that gender concerns influence the themes she addresses.

During my research at Agudath Or, Rina became a grandmother for the first time. My visits occurred during a momentous period for her, one whose excitement I was privileged to observe. She arrived straight from the hospital, where she had been up all night awaiting the birth of her grandson, to teach the first Shabbat morning Torah study group I attended. The two prominent metaphors that she used to describe being a teacher and teaching—an umbilical cord and a midwife—were influenced by the events taking place in her private life. They provide insight into the vital nexus between the personal and the communal that suffuses Rina's approach to teaching adults.

Places, People, Philosophies

At the time of our interviews Rina had been a rabbi at Temple Agudath Or for twenty-two years. It was her only congregation since she became a rabbi in her early thirties. Before attending rabbinical school at Hebrew Union College, she worked as a Jewish educator in a Conservative synagogue's religious school and as a teacher in a Jewish day school in Southern California. Rina's personal, educational, and professional biography reveals an ongoing immersion in Jewish communal life and Jewish learning. She was raised in a traditional household. Her father had been a congregational rabbi for many years and was an accomplished professor of Jewish Studies. Her mother was also a scholar and teacher of Judaism. Rina treasures the experience of growing up in a household steeped in Jewish rituals and rhythms. In her private life she still leans more to traditional religious practice despite her ordination as a Reform rabbi. Teaching adults about the Jewish home and Jewish family rituals was a recurring theme during our interviews and in my observations. Although she never described herself in this way, Rina regularly incorporates the perspective of a Jewish wife, mother, and, more recently, grandmother into her teaching.

Rina also spoke about the centrality of Jewish summer camp as a formative influence on her Jewish identity. Immersion in a Jewish community that extended beyond her nuclear family provided her with early and ongoing exposure throughout adolescence and early adulthood to the communal energy that undergirds Judaism. Creating community is another significant theme in Rina's rabbinate and one of the central aims of her teaching. As a young adult, she worked in a synagogue with a rabbi whose beliefs about community helped her further articulate the holistic understanding of it she absorbed while a camper. Jewish community for Rina is more than a group of people who congregate in one place. It is an active orientation toward the world—more of a verb than a noun. People ideally bring their "psyche and heart and spirit and intellect" to it.[2] Making connections among those dimensions of our lives is the very essence of the Jewish communal experience in Rina's view.

In her path toward becoming a rabbi, Rina cited two other individuals who influenced her evolution. Jessica Davids was one of the first generation of women ordained in the Reform movement. She was also the first woman rabbi whom Rina knew well. Rina described her as an "open, unafraid thinker." Rina models this disposition in her own teaching. Confronting her learners with open-ended questions and encouraging them to ask their own difficult ones functions as a fundamental teaching strategy for Rina. She credits Jessica with showing her how to be this kind of a rabbinic teacher. Finally, Rina's husband, himself a leader and educator in the

---

2. I interviewed Rina three times between November 29, 2007 and January 17, 2008. All future interview references occurred during these interviews.

American Jewish community, although not a rabbi, heartily supported her decision to become a rabbi. He also inspired her to refine her conception of teaching adults. She learned from him that finding out what kinds of questions adults needed to ask, hear, and discuss was at the heart of successful teaching. To frame study with adults around their questions rather than her agenda or subjects she chooses is fundamental to her teaching.

Teacher of the Community

Before she became a rabbi Rina was a Jewish educator. That earlier career shapes her conception of her rabbinic role as a teacher. Rather than viewing her rabbinate as a qualitatively distinctive professional path or status transformation, she sees it as an extension of her prior work as a Jewish educator. As a rabbi, she is able to "broaden the circle of influence" she had already established as a teacher or as a principal in a synagogue's religious school. From her rabbinic post she is able to articulate a communal vision of education whose impact can extend in ever-widening circles.

Rina's role as a teacher of adults is embedded in her description of herself as a "teacher of the community." Rina wants education to influence all areas of congregational life. She accompanies her adult congregants as they delve into Jewish learning. She hopes that such study extends to other domains of Jewish living in a way that infuses their lives with wholeness. Feeling connected to the rhythms of their synagogue is a vital conduit for such a process. One of her learners shared with me an exquisitely apt image of the synagogue community that she heard Rina use more than once: the front porch of a family home. On the front porch the family gathers publicly. Neighbors walk by and stop to chat. Hospitality is extended to visitors. Social intercourse is informal, sought after, and valued. People get to know each other through the regularity of meeting each other again and again. This same learner mentioned that Rina's house is only a short walk from the synagogue. She invites learners to her home throughout the year. She and her husband show films in their garden during the summer. Friendships develop over the years that tie learners to each other and to Rina through such efforts.

THE ANNUAL RETREAT—"AGUDATH OR AT ITS BEST"

Rina's sense of herself as a teacher of the community influenced the creation of what is known at Agudath Or as "The Annual Retreat." The retreat is a defining feature of the synagogue's collective identity. The story of its origins and purposes is another example of Rina's holistic ideas about Jewish education. The retreat originally started as an extension of adult learning. Rather than import a scholar-in-residence to spend a weekend lecturing at the synagogue, Rina and her lay organizers decided that its goal would be to gather a group of adults for an intensive opportunity to live Shabbat and learn together for several days offsite. A congregant who subsequently became a rabbi helped Rina plan the first retreat. Since then, it has grown into a synagogue-wide, multigenerational, lay-led village in miniature every Memorial Day weekend. Attendees teach each other. Synagogue educators and clergy also teach and learn. In Rina's language, there is no "Great Giver of Information." Rather, everyone becomes "givers and receivers" in a deliberately egalitarian setup. Close to two hundred people come together year in and year out. Children who grew up attending the retreat return as college students to participate as young adults. To Rina, it is the primary example of empowering the adults in her synagogue to create Jewish community through teaching and learning. In our discussions Rina frequently connected the words "teaching" and "empowering" together. It was one of the reasons that she stressed the symbolic and real educational value of the Annual Retreat for her adult congregants.

Not long before our interviews, Rina had recast her rabbinic responsibilities at Agudath Or. A feeling of dissatisfaction with her position prompted the change. She had wondered whether it was time to move on. She realized, however, that leaving Agudath Or for another synagogue would not ensure a change. Instead, she started to imagine how she might put more of her energy into her ideas about education because they lay at the heart of her rabbinic identity. Over an extended period of consultation with her husband, her rabbinic colleague, and the Board of Trustees, she arrived at a restructuring of her position. She became the rabbi in charge of synagogue education overall. This has meant that she works more closely with the various Jewish educators on the staff to conceptualize curriculum and programs. She also has primary responsibility for formulating the synagogue's educational "metaquestions." That is the term she employed to refer to the broad educational concerns the congregation faces. In this capacity she is the rabbi who connects different parts of the synagogue through education. In her new position Rina certainly continues to teach content to her learners. What became clearer as she transitioned to her new role was that more important to her than any particular text or topic, however, is introducing congregants to a process of active involvement in Jewish life. This happens best in Rina's eyes through serious and ongoing Jewish learning. While the Annual Retreat epitomizes such a process, her day-to-day efforts act as the primary locus through which she keeps it alive.

CONNECTION

"Connection" is a concept critical to Rina. She mentioned it repeatedly in our interviews. Many of her congregants did so, too, when they spoke with me. During the course of our interviews, and in several brief e-mail exchanges subsequent to them, Rina drew on two evocative birth metaphors that attempted to capture more clearly what she intends by connection: an umbilical cord and a midwife.

In the former, a rabbi's role is to help connect people to Jewish wisdom through teaching. Indeed, for Rina, teaching involves "connecting Jews to the source of life, to the power of God's presence, to community, to religious ritual, to Jewish texts and the wisdom and stories they contain." Rina returned to the power of birth-related metaphors at other times in my research. Instead of drawing upon the umbilical-cord metaphor, she spoke at length about how the image of herself as a midwife reflects even more compellingly a teaching-learning partnership between rabbi and congregants. She wants to be a facilitator of learning. The congregants discover through study how to "give birth" to ongoing connections with Judaism. She accompanies them as a knowledgeable, caring, and involved companion. She guides them to their own discoveries, ones that only they can bring forth.

Rina acknowledged that the birth of her first grandchild affected her choice of metaphors. Her status change from mother to grandmother sent her back in time to her own experiences of childbirth. The feeling of holding a newborn baby brought feelings to life that were both familiar to her as the mother of four children and new, because it had been a long time since she had held a baby in her arms. These metaphors also stimulated her to reflect on the vulnerability and the excitement at the heart of Jewish learning. She spoke about the power of a teacher's influence in an adult's life. The metaphors reminded her forcefully of her teaching philosophy. As a rabbi she teaches as an authoritative helper—a connector—not as the main attraction. It is why teaching, learning, and adult empowerment are concepts powerfully entwined with each other.

RINA'S COURSES

At Agudath Or Rina's conception of adult Jewish education promotes intellectual openness, spiritual connection, and belonging to a close-knit community. A significant part of Rina's work involves teaching a diverse group of courses that seek to fulfill these aims. During her tenure at Agudath Or, Rina has organized courses on a range of subjects. She has designed these courses by assessing the learning needs of her congregants and through an ongoing conversation with her current adult learners about their interests. During my year of observation, Rina engaged in the following kinds of formal teaching (in order of frequency):

- A weekly Torah study session on Shabbat morning that she organized soon after arriving at the synagogue two decades ago. It is attended by approximately forty people, primarily in their sixties to eighties, roughly divided between men and women. Rina mentioned that she was concerned that this class was no longer attracting younger members of the congregation. At the time of our interviews, she was thinking about changes in the structure that would help bring in new participants.

- A biweekly adult Bar and Bat Mitzvah class that met at her home in the evenings. It required a two-year commitment, culminating in a special Shabbat morning Torah-reading service led by the participants, during which they celebrate their becoming an adult Bar or Bat Mitzvah. Approximately fifteen people attended, ranging in age from thirty to over eighty, the majority of whom were women. In previous years, there were more often equal numbers of men and women.

- A biweekly "Introduction to Spiritual Questions" class that was starting as I concluded my observations.

- A once-a-month, early-morning women's group called "Breakfast and Learn" on topics of interest to women. It has been in existence for more than a decade. Attendees ranged in age from their forties to their eighties, with approximately twenty participants.

- A four-times-a-year women's book group on diverse topics relevant to Judaism and Jewish life, which she co-teaches with a member of the synagogue who is an ordained rabbi or other adult educator colleagues. This course includes a retreat, at which time the group's participants go away for a weekend of intensive study led by Rina. The group has been in existence for a decade and includes women who range in age from their thirties to their eighties. Approximately thirty women attended each session.
- Multiple adult learning sessions with parents from the religious school on thematic topics, as part of grade-level family-education programs held throughout the year. Rina has organized these classes and chosen their themes since assuming oversight of the religious school. According to Rina they achieve almost 100 percent attendance by the parents.

The learning in all of these groups includes an informal social component. Attendees had ample time to chat, eat, and drink before or after learning. Rina taught several of the classes in her home or at those of congregants. Inviting learners into her home and teaching in the homes of her congregants is one way that Rina succeeds in turning teaching and learning into an opportunity to create closer bonds. Her willingness to bridge the distance between the personal spaces of people's homes and the public milieu of the synagogue points to sensitivity about the influence of physical settings in adult learning. It is one that is worthy of further research related to adult learning in congregations.

THEMES IN RINA'S TEACHING

Truths Not the Truth

One of my earliest observations of Rina occurred on the Shabbat morning just after Thanksgiving. At nine o'clock I walked into the picturesque "Chapel in the Woods" (the name given to a smaller sanctuary distinct from the main building). A few people were there. In the alcove area at the front of the building, food and beverages were laid out. As attendees began to arrive they noticed me, a newcomer. Several approached me and introduced themselves. Most of the people I spoke with were in their sixties and seventies. They had known Rina for at least a decade. Some had been learning with her since her arrival at the synagogue.

On my return visits to the Shabbat morning Torah study, the regular attendees recognized me and asked about my research. Many shared that their Jewish education as adults had begun in Shabbat study with Rina. It then branched out to other courses she taught and to other educational experiences with her, such as trips to Israel and Europe. Recurrent themes in these informal exchanges were that Rina nurtured their learning. She welcomed learners where they were. Especially, she did not give to or expect from students preconceived responses. Many learners called this giving "The Right Answer." They attended Shabbat Torah study because they felt impelled to ask difficult questions about Jewish theology and Jewish history. They noted Rina's ability to provoke reflection among them through the bold questions she raises. She encourages them to follow her lead. From her they have learned to understand Judaism as a sophisticated and evolving religious system.

Rina spoke about the Shabbat study group as people who "share a universe." Not long after her arrival at Agudath Or, the senior rabbi at that time suggested that she start a parallel service in the small chapel that had been recently constructed. The group began with a handful of adults who gathered in the alcove of the entryway to study together, pause for an *oneg* (festive gathering with food and beverages), and then come together for prayer and more study. The group took nine years to go through the Pentateuch. During that time it expanded to more than forty participants. Although Rina has been considering ways to attract younger participants, she also views the group's longevity as a powerful part of the congregation's history of commitment to adult learning. Over the years they completed the Pentateuch, began it again, and studied Song of Songs, Ruth, Lamentations, Ecclesiastes, and Esther. During my observations they were in the middle of Kings. Along with studying these sacred texts, the group incorporates secular approaches into the learning, such as a unit on turning points in Jewish history using primary sources and books on biblical criticism.

Difficult topics, such as the nature of religious truth and the relationship between faith and reason, are central themes they return to continually. These subjects reveal the intellectual, religious, spiritual, and existential concerns of Rina and her learners. Sacred and secular texts become springboards for examining deeper issues of interest to the group. Questions about the role of history in Judaism, the place of Jewish philosophy in sacred learning, and the relationship between secular and religious ways of understanding Judaism and Jewish tradition frequently get addressed.

The Midwife

The group members share their personal experiences, their intellectual reflections, their confusion, and their frustration. Rina encourages them to do so respectfully, honestly, and openly. Over the years, a storehouse of questions has generated insights and memories as the group endeavors collaboratively to find answers to their individual questions.

For more than twenty years the Shabbat Torah study group has met every Shabbat morning. While new people have joined, those who came at the beginning remain devoted participants. The experience of learning together over so many years creates a familiarity among the learners that extends beyond their belonging to the same congregation. The group has evolved its own internal narrative. At the heart of their story is a willingness to confront the complexity of an ancient tradition in its encounter with their modern lives. The mutual respect for one another's opinions makes honesty possible. Rina related to me how only on one occasion could she remember the group becoming visibly irritated—toward a visitor. A rabbi from one of the more conservative ideological streams of Judaism taught as a guest scholar. In response to a question from one of the learners he naively said, "The answer is . . . " En masse the attendees objected to his choice of the word "the." During their years of learning they had arrived at an understanding that there is no one correct answer to any religious question. Their stance illustrated a core value that animates their group. It is what makes it possible to expose their ideas and feelings about topics as vast and complex as whether it is necessary to believe in God to be a Jew and the relationship of the modern State of Israel to the Israel depicted in the Bible.

During my first observation of the Shabbat Torah study, I was intrigued by the way Rina interacted with a learner who requested clarification about whether it was possible to know "the truth." In our interview following that visit I asked Rina to elaborate on her response. I was especially curious about why she avoided giving a direct answer to the learner. Rina's response opened a window into her orientation to teaching religion. She explained that the question of "the truth" or "truths" is a frequent theme she addresses. As a rabbi she rejects the idea that any human being or any humanly created system knows "the truth" as an absolute and objective reality. In her words, "Once you know the truth, and you can wrap yourself around it, you are bigger than God because you own the truth . . . And I've quoted for them millions of times Larry Kushner's brilliant rewrite of the first of the Ten Commandments: 'I'm God. You're not.' . . . Different people know different truths. Different systems know different truths. These are all aspects of a truth which is not knowable. That's how I teach."

Rina's belief that religion and religious questions need to be explored from a multiplicity of perspectives is one of the reasons why she encourages her learners to ask questions that do not have yes or no answers. She asks those kinds of questions and models how to expand the range of thinking about any religious question. In explaining this approach, she referred to her rabbinic mentor from the synagogue in California. For him all kinds of questions were open for discussion. There were no taboos. When I asked Rina to clarify why that was so important to her, she answered by reiterating how religion needed to be part of one's entire experience of the world: "This way it's connected to everything that is." Her approach to truth and questions does not lead Rina to espouse a radically relativistic worldview. Rather, it allows her learners to engage with Judaism in a way that invites them to take it as seriously as they would other parts of their identity. If her adult learners hold diverse values and beliefs about family, childrearing, sexuality, politics, and the environment that are shaped by their histories and experiences, why should it be any different with Judaism? On the contrary, to explore Judaism with an open mind and heart can model how to proceed in other parts of their lives as well. This is a potentially transformative journey that Rina takes with her learners. She does not stand above or separate from them. While she may have arrived already at her own understandings, they are not set in stone. Nor does she see it as educationally beneficial to impose her conclusions on her learners. Part of studying together is being present to learning from them as they go through their own voyages of discovery.

Relationships and Rituals

Rina's perspective on multiple truths leads her learners to questions that move well beyond exclusively intellectual issues. They delve into personal domains. How does religious life help or harm us in our relationships with ourselves and with other people? The interpersonal and intrapersonal focus of Rina's teaching is another dominant strand of her teaching.

During my year at Agudath Or, Rina was in the middle of a two-year cycle of an adult Bar and Bat Mitzvah class that would culminate in a celebratory Shabbat service in the spring. In Rina's initial meeting with me before our interviews she invited me to attend the upcoming class. It was held every other Tuesday evening at her home. Rina divulged her worries about the group. In spite of already meeting for a year, the participants demonstrated little cohesiveness or closeness. People still did not know each other's names. Attendance was irregular. In her many years of teaching the course, this was the first time she faced such a situation. It perplexed and upset her. She had decided to raise these worries with the group at the next meeting. She suggested that I give her feedback during our subsequent interview if I saw anything that might help. Rather than ask me to come to a class where she might showcase her teaching, she seemed curious and interested to include me when things were less than perfect.

That evening I observed Rina's honesty as an educator. In her living room the participants sat on chairs and sofas and heard her communicate her concerns. I watched as the learners volunteered their perspectives. I listened as they brainstormed ways during the class and outside of the scheduled course times that they could get to know each other better. Toward the end of the session, Rina explained one of her core teaching principles: Without processing there is no learning. This is one of Rina's mantras as an educator. By "processing" she means the ability to reflect on the learning experience with the group. She solicits the learners' feelings toward the material and toward the quality of the learning. In the absence of such collaborative reflection, learning gets stymied. Put positively, reflection encourages engagement. Afterward, Rina said that she was more hopeful that the group would coalesce in a positive direction.

Several weeks later I followed up with her about the class. While she remained less positive about this cohort than previous ones, progress had been made. She saw an improved commitment to regular attendance. Several of the participants had begun to meet with each other outside of the class. Rina also wondered out loud to me whether the lack of connectedness derived in part from the focus she brought to the group. She pondered whether she needed to take a break after teaching it for so many years. Was it possible that the lack of connection she observed was due in part to her own lower energy level? She sensed intuitively that the spirit she brought to her teaching influenced the learners' experiences. As such, she felt compelled to examine her own attitudes rather than look only to the participants' behaviors. Introspection about her relationship to the material and to her learners formed an essential part of how she evaluated the success of her teaching. Throughout my time with her, I noticed how important it was to Rina to honestly critique her own attitudes, considering how they might affect the dynamic in any group she taught.

Rina's emphasis on the interpersonal nature of her rabbinic role is complex. While she stresses the need for genuine relationships with her learners, she accepts that as a congregational rabbi a certain distance must remain intact. Through pastoral meetings with many of her congregants, she knows a great deal about them. As a result she is involved in their lives in a way that they are not, and cannot be in hers, because she is their rabbi. For an educator who views Judaism as fundamentally constructed on connectedness to community and spirituality, her rabbinic position entails setting boundaries between her public persona and her private life. Personal stories she relates, times when she opens her home, and private dilemmas she encounters must all be considered carefully before being shared publicly. The closeness even of adult friendships is an uneven one between a rabbi and a congregant-learner. As a result, Rina recognizes that connecting to her learners cannot be the primary aim of her teaching. Instead, fostering such closeness among the learners assumes a dominant place in her teaching. Here, too, she grasps that as an adult educator being a facilitator aligns best with her emphasis on interpersonal relationships.

I attended Rina's adult Bar and Bat Mitzvah class on two further occasions: once during Hanukkah at her home, and once when they made a visit to a *mikvah* (ritual bath) located in a nearby Conservative synagogue. During these visits, and in further observations of and discussions with her, I realized that building interpersonal bonds with fellow learners and congregants represents only one aspect of Rina's attentiveness to relationships. Another dimension involves the kinds of relationships that adults develop with Jewish tradition through ritual practice. In one of our interviews Rina spoke about the power of ritual being grounded in "what it means to do the same thing in a predictable way at a predictable time, and how it is that it anchors a person in the universe." She shared several crucial personal stories about how Jewish rituals function in her life. She includes these stories when she teaches about ritual. As a rabbinic educator she works to bring the rituals to life through intergenerational experiential learning. Such programs as the Annual Retreat and Synaplex, (part of a nationwide program created by STAR [Synagogues: Transformation and Renewal] to invigorate Shabbat at synagogues throughout the country) are synagogue-wide opportunities to simultaneously blend learning about ritual with living it. Synaplex draws hundreds of congregants once a month for a Friday night of prayer, learning, cultural programs, and celebration.

The Midwife

According to Rina, for the membership of Agudath Or the congregation, rather than the home, is the environment where Jewish ritual commitments find concrete expression. The synagogue is the primary Jewish address for many of her congregants because of the attenuated nature of Jewish ritual observance among most of them. Although she expressed some disappointment that the majority of her congregants do not experience a home rich with Jewish religious ritual, she accepts it as a reality. Nonetheless, she pursues ritual observance as a core focus of her teaching. When she discussed Shabbat with her adult Bar and Bat Mitzvah students, for example, she explained to them, "It is bucking the entire culture to do it. I grew up with it, so it's easy. But it is a huge counterculture thing to do. We don't have to be at the beck and call of everybody else. It takes a lot of family strength. Having friends who support you makes it a lot easier. It's not on a scale of zero to one hundred. There are different ways to do Shabbat." She mentioned to the group that a few years earlier the synagogue leadership decided to shift the time of their Friday night service from the traditional Reform eight o'clock to six o'clock. The goal was to allow families to return home at a reasonable hour to share a Shabbat dinner, rather than being rushed to get to a service.

As much as she teaches the value of Jewish home rituals, she believes that Agudath Or itself must be a home to her congregants. It needs to be the place where ritual connects them to Judaism and to one another. If they do not celebrate Shabbat in the privacy of their homes, Agudath Or invites them to try it out communally. A question that she posed to her Bar and Bar Mitzvah learners during their study of Shabbat resonated with me long after I heard her ask it of them: "How do we as Reform Jews create a community of celebrants when we are all making our individual choices?"

Rina described herself to me as a liberal Jew who grew up in a traditional Conservative household. Her parents infused their home with the rhythms of Jewish ritual. Her Jewish identity was powerfully influenced by Jewish observance. Yet as a rabbi of a Reform congregation whose members minimally observe Jewish home rituals, Rina's way of teaching her adult learners about this facet of Jewish life did not come across as grounded in any sense of divinely ordained commandment. Rina teaches ritual through the lenses of history, psychology, sociology, and spirituality rather than via the mandates of Jewish law. Her criticism of fundamentalism in religion dovetails with her flexibility regarding the manner in which traditional rituals can be practiced. Her stance helps her speak and teach ritual in a nonjudgmental and imaginative voice to her learners instead of a coercive one.

To Rina, ritual offers us a chance, in her words, to "bring you back to where you want to be." From this perspective, rituals become a creative pathway toward a spirituality founded on connectedness to an ancient religious tradition. Sacred rituals hold the reciprocal potential to both ground and renew people and a tradition through every generation's involvement with them. Rina reiterated this orientation in an address she gave to parents at the annual open house for the religious school in the fall of 2008. She referred to Judaism's ability to "nurture a sense of empathy and human connection." She spoke about finding a meaning and a mission in life as the natural inheritance of Jewish children. She followed with several concrete suggestions about how to draw on Jewish ritual to cultivate a sense of "being a whole person." Prominent among these included creating sacred time. In particular she discussed Shabbat. She related several stories about Shabbat in her own nuclear family, emphasizing along the way that "it has been the greatest gift to my family." She described the benefits of consecrating time on Friday evening for family. Part of that experience included "holding kids, telling them you love them with a traditional blessing or your own words, making time for husbands and wives to acknowledge their love for each other in front of their children." All of these behaviors reflect traditional Shabbat ritual behavior. But Rina broadened their implications by indicating explicitly how they might enrich family relationships. She concluded by adding that Agudath Or could help families develop deeper ritual observance should they desire it. She warmly invited the parents to attend Shabbat events sponsored by the synagogue.

Given her support for traditional rituals, albeit sensitively adapted to the contemporary realities of her congregants, I was intrigued by her drive to introduce adult learners to the more perplexing and even troubling parts of Jewish tradition. When I queried Rina about the potential contradiction, her answer was tentative but coherent. She imagined these two aspects of her teaching as part of a dialectical process. The ritual grounds people in relationships and in the world more generally. Being centered in such a way liberates us to ask hard questions about faith and belief without being "untethered" by them. Rina saw this as a necessary process in order for the adults in her congregation to integrate intellectual, spiritual, and experiential dimensions into a Jewish way of living. She referred to two periods in her life when she underwent a crisis of faith in Judaism. One happened before and one not long after she became a rabbi. Both concerned the misogynist tendencies in traditional Judaism. These crises threatened to severely undermine her identity as a Jew and as a rabbi.

They did not, in the end, damage her fundamental conviction that Jewish ritual and tradition act as anchors in a person's life. I asked her how she resolved these painful episodes. She answered with great frankness, drawing on a metaphor that resonated with the central place relationships occupy in her rabbinic identity:

> I think it was pretty internal, and in the way you find a way to cope with the negative things you find out about yourself or about people you love. You find a way to deal with it, to say that the system is far from perfect. It's people's best attempts to understand the divine, and people make a lot of mistakes, and that revelation is not over. It's ongoing and this is work we need to do.

As Rina explained to her adult Bar and Bat Mitzvah group, "Without processing there is no learning." To process involves learning how to critically reflect on our beliefs and behaviors. It echoes ideas supported by research on adult learning by such scholars as Stephen Brookfield, Patricia Cranton, and Jack Mezirow (see chapter 1). To be able to create cognitive distance from our loyalties and commitments without abandoning them is the kind of work that constructive-developmental psychologist Robert Kegan argued lies at the heart of postmodern adult development. Through her attention to relationships in the context of adult learning, Rina enters into some of the most vital debates about the meaning not only of Jewish learning in the twenty-first century, but also about adult development more generally.

Sharing Stories

Rina aspires to guide her adult learners to connect Jewish learning to all of life. As a teacher she works hard to create a productive tension between intellectual daring and emotional depth. This aim reflects Rina's conviction that Judaism helps an individual "become a whole person." One of the key ways that Rina mediates the potentially conflicting outcomes of the dialogue between mind and heart is via stories. Stories become a way to describe, frame, analyze, and model this ongoing process. Although she includes stories as a means, in her words, of "tapping into the wisdom of tradition and of our community," it was particularly prominent as a deliberate teaching strategy in her work with parents of children enrolled in the religious school.

Rina works closely with the religious school principal (who is also a member of Agudath Or and who began her involvement in Jewish education at the synagogue through her participation in organizing the Annual Retreat). Together they define the overarching goals of the religious school. With Rina's guidance, the religious school has transformed its curriculum to emphasize Jewish culture rather than Hebrew-language acquisition skills and text study. Enculturation is its aim. "Enculturation" is a term the Jewish education scholar Isa Aron coined to distinguish between an instructional model of religious education and one that emphasizes above all "a loving induction into the Jewish culture and the Jewish community" as primary (Aron 1995, 68).

Enculturation best describes the religious school model at Agudath Or. The changed approach represented a substantive shift in the orientation and aims of the religious school. Rina oversaw the evolution. Part of the transformation included creating regular family education programs at the religious school. The new curriculum now incorporates an independent adult learning segment that is integrated into family education programs. Rina teaches the adults. Doing so gives her another forum for reaching adult congregants. At least twice a year for each grade (K–7), parents are encouraged to attend family education programs. Since many of the parents have children in multiple grades, they often come at least four times a year to spend a morning studying together at the synagogue. The programs achieve almost full attendance. These adults get to know Rina as a teacher of adults rather than only as a pulpit rabbi or a pastoral counselor. Although they are short-term learning opportunities, they become a vehicle, perhaps underutilized by Rina and her colleagues, whereby parents of school-age children are exposed to adult learning at Agudath Or.

Rina's work with this adult cohort demonstrates how she intentionally incorporates stories from Jewish tradition and stories from people's lives (including her own) into her teaching. More specifically, these learning opportunities often focus on Torah narratives that have a family component to them. They become a vehicle for exploring Judaism in light of participants' most intimate and close personal relationships. When I asked Rina for an example of one such experience, she offered the following anecdote:

> This Sunday our second graders have a program called "What's in a Name?" We will be studying the story about Jacob and Esau both

seeking their father Isaac's blessing. The hope is to connect what their kids are learning—the birth stories of the matriarchs and patriarchs—with their own birth stories, so that Torah remains a way to understand your own life and think about your own life. It's also a chance to think about how parents give blessings to their children, and how our relationships with them influence those blessings. It also serves a purpose of having parents and children talk together, again empowering people to talk together about things that matter. And making sure that kids have their Hebrew name early on. It's one of several times that we have the programs. Teaching is teaching the adults Torah, but also teaching how to read Torah, teaching that Torah has a connection to your life, teaching parents to talk to their children about these things. That's teaching.

Here Rina offered her process for utilizing biblical narratives. She exposes adults to content, some of which they have heard about but probably never studied. She introduces them to the complexity of the narratives of the matriarchs and patriarchs. She invites them to consider how the themes resonate in their lives as parents, Jews, and as human beings.

A close correlation existed between Rina's earlier description of this class in our interviews and the way she presented the material when I observed her teach it a second time, a year later, with a new group of parents. I was struck by the frontal nature of Rina's teaching in this setting. It seemed prompted by the parents' lack of familiarity with one another and with the material. The participants asked Rina many basic questions about the narrative. They seemed surprised and unsettled by the rivalry and favoritism displayed in the biblical narrative. It was unclear, however, whether Rina achieved her intended goal of opening up windows into their own experiences. The lack of follow up discussion, as exists in most of her other adult education courses, showed the limits of short-term encounters in terms of evaluating the quality of the learning.

NOT LIKE RABBIS I GREW UP WITH

As part of her opening address to the parents of the religious school at the annual open house in 2008, Rina narrated a condensed history of her own family. She shared stories about family members (no longer alive) who suffered from addiction and its effects on the family. She divulged several of her own childrearing errors. She proceeded to explain why she chose to share these personal anecdotes. To the audience of approximately around two hundred adults, she said, "I'm a rabbi, but I don't have a perfect family. I don't want you to idealize my family. I don't believe there are any formulas for successful parenting. But we can use Jewish life to nurture us and our children."

This kind of self-disclosure is a distinctive motif in Rina's teaching. It helps overcome the distance between a rabbi and her congregants. She speaks to them as an adult who struggles as they do to make sense of her decisions and experiences as a parent. She draws on Judaism as a guide and invites them to contemplate this possibility, too. During the open house the group watched a documentary called "Who Are the Debolts?" The film tells the story of a couple who adopted a dozen severely handicapped children. It explores the questions of "What makes a person whole? What makes a family?" After it concluded, Rina opened the floor for feedback. A torrent of brief and highly personal stories ensued. After listening to all of them, Rina responded by speaking once again from her own experiences as a parent. She mentioned in passing the ways that Jewish tradition had helped support her children's development and the closeness of their family.

Even in a large setting such as this one, Rina's storytelling bridges the distance that can exist between a rabbi and her congregants. She encourages them to see her as a rabbi capable of empathizing with their parental concerns. She positions herself as a guide who will help them navigate their evolving participation in the Jewish education of their children in the synagogue. The stories she tells, teaches, and hears introduce congregants in a very personal way to their rabbi rather than as a distant leader.

Parents of children in the religious school are one cohort whose particular needs Rina pays careful attention to in her teaching. It is not the only one. During our interviews Rina did not emphasize her status as one of the first generation of women in the rabbinate. It became clear, however, that certain classes and topics reflected her willingness to address issues that may be of special concern to women, providing a forum in her congregation for women to study and discuss these topics together.

More than a decade ago Rina created, and subsequently has taught, co-taught, and participated in the Women's Book Group and in the Women's Breakfast Study group at Agudath Or. In each of these groups, Rina co-ordinates topics and books that the adult learners want to explore together. In the case of the former group, Rina and her colleagues select a book that addresses a Jewish topic or theme. The participants meet four times during the year. Their learning culminates with a weekend retreat, during which they pursue intensive study with Rina in an immersive communal setting. The latter group was initially created for women who worked outside the home to meet before the workday began. It has evolved into a cohort open to all women in the congregation that addresses diverse topics of special interest to women on a monthly basis. In both settings, Rina's presence as a teacher is critical. She also team-teaches with a synagogue colleague, with a congregant, or with a guest educator.

In informal interviews, the learners in these groups emphasized that Rina's ability to see issues as a woman, a mother, and a wife drew them to her. A participant in the book group, a woman in her fifties, described Rina as a rabbi who "makes connections as a woman, who talks about topics that I can connect to, who raises subjects relevant to women, family matters, personal relationships. She is not like the rabbis I grew up with. She talks about topics that are close to my heart." Remarks such as this one highlight Rina's ability to teach about Judaism in a way that heightens connection to learning in a personal way. Rina never mentioned feminism or feminist theory during our interviews, but my observations and her learners' responses demonstrated that gender concerns clearly affect her teaching in these contexts. Both of these women's study groups draw old-timers and newer members. The more recent participants find their way to the groups through word of mouth or through notices in the synagogue newsletters and on the website. Each group attracts as many as thirty-five participants for any session.

During my year of observation, the book group finished Simon Wiesenthal's book *The Sunflower: On the Possibilities and Limits of Forgiveness*; they began reading *My Grandfather's Blessings*, authored by a Jewish psychiatrist named Rachel Naomi Remen. It was a memoir from which Rina had read excerpts at one of the previous women's retreats. After the retreat, two of the women in the group consulted Rina about using it as a book-group selection. The process of inviting input from the learners and welcoming learners' involvement about choosing material exemplifies Rina's focus on collaboration as part of the learning process. Although the book does not address exclusively Jewish topics, Rina helped the group link its themes with Jewish ones, especially those relating to spirituality.

Her willingness to openly discuss matters such as family relations, sexuality, and cancer in the context of this book may be what some of the women learners meant when they talked about Rina's ability to connect to congregants in a way that distinguished her from other clergy they knew. As one of the members of the book group remarked, "Rina draws people out through weaving her scholarly knowledge, her stories of the tradition and her own personal life, freeing people to do that also."

BIRTHING CONNECTIONS

Rina's role as an adult educator points to a strong focus on helping her learners holistically integrate Judaism into their lives. Ongoing learning in their community enables personal relationships to grow out of and, in turn, bolster such learning. Transmission of content serves a purpose far beyond accumulating Jewish content knowledge. Instead, learning gives birth to attachments to Agudath Or, to Jewish tradition, and to Rina as the rabbi who accompanies such creative interconnectedness. Adult Jewish study serves the development of individuals for whom thinking, feeling, and doing in a Jewish context draws them into a safe communal space and motivates them to grow as adults. This is what Rina and her learners mean when they speak of connections.

Throughout our interviews Rina repeatedly stressed that she neither wants to be, nor sees herself, as the "Great Giver of Information." Rather, as she wrote in one of her e-mail messages to me, her most essential role is that of facilitator of learning. As she prefers to describe herself, she is a midwife to her community. The highly personalized and penetrating teacher-learner and learner-learner exchanges that result from translating this identity into practice offer a miniature model of the kind of community she seeks to create for Agudath Or as a whole. To a very great degree she has worked to fulfill in her own way and in her own synagogue the aspirations of her rabbinic mentor. He urged his clergy colleagues from all Jewish denominations to transform their synagogues into communities where teaching and learning lead to close relationships and personal enrichment. Over the past two-plus decades Rabbi Rina Lewin's role as a teacher of adults demonstrates that his exhortation is more than a dream.

chapter 4

THE LEARNER

A synagogue of approximately 850 households founded in 1908, the thriving congregation of Beth Shalom[1] celebrated its one hundredth anniversary in 2008. Beth Shalom's building is an imposing brick structure, perched on the hillside corner of a busy suburban road and a quiet side street. Behind the security desk in the entryway, a door leads to a glass-enclosed administrative area that includes Senior Rabbi Eric Miller's office. Two assistant rabbis, a cantor, and the directors of congregational learning, family education, and the religious school compose his synagogue team. He has led the congregation since 1994.

When I asked both Jewish professionals and laypeople to identify a congregational rabbi whom they considered to be an outstanding teacher, a vast majority named Rabbi Miller. Yet an initial attempt to include him in my study failed. When I contacted him in the fall of 2007, he explained that in addition to his regular commitments, Beth Shalom was at the start of their centennial year of celebration. Other time-consuming projects loomed. His busy schedule, even more packed than it usually was, precluded further engagements. Because of the high regard I heard about his teaching, however, I remained persuaded that another attempt was worthwhile. Ten months later, in July 2008, I contacted him again. This time he agreed to participate.[2]

---

1. A pseudonym. "Beth Shalom" translates into English as "House of Peace."
2. I interviewed Eric at Beth Shalom three times between July 29, 2008 and August 28, 2008. All future interview references occurred during that time. Weekly observations between September 2008 and January 2009 followed.

MEETING ERIC

For our interviews Eric led me to his office located at the very end of a narrow corridor. It was a modest space. A desk, a computer, two small sofas, a coffee table, full bookshelves, a white writing board on one wall, and windows with closed blinds facing the main street gave it an almost claustrophobic feel. The room suggested the compact and somewhat cramped quarters of the captain of a big ship. Indeed, at well over six feet tall, physically fit, sporting a walrus mustache, and bearing the ruddy complexion of a person who spends ample time outdoors, it was not impossible for me to imagine Eric holding such a position. During the workweek he dressed casually in khaki pants, sneakers, and collar shirts worn without a tie, while on Shabbat and holidays his suited attired reflected the change from mundane to sacred time.

In his late fifties at the time of my research, Eric does not conform easily to any conventional stereotypes of rabbis. He distinctly remembers that as a freckled, redheaded boy growing up in a major metropolitan city with a large Irish population, he blended in easily with his Irish neighbors. He recalled how, as a five-year-old, he accompanied his mother, also fair in complexion, to sign up for kindergarten at a neighborhood Orthodox school. The man who greeted them glanced at Eric and his mother somewhat skeptically. He said to them, "You know that this is a Jewish school?" Eric looked different phenotypically from his Jewish classmates because of his hair color, facial complexion, and above-average height. He also quickly differentiated himself from them because of his precocious academic ability. In elementary school he rapidly skipped two grades, a situation that he found trying socially when he reached middle school.

Eric did not mention these early memories in the context of his current position. Yet the sense of his being immersed in a Jewish community on the one hand, while distinguishing himself there, on the other hand, has been a consistent motif in his Jewish experience. It remains so in his rabbinate. Congregants referred to him as being unlike other congregational rabbis they knew. They attributed this uniqueness in part to his luminous intelligence. Equally significant to them, however, was that neither his scholarly knowledge nor his intellectual acumen made him inaccessible. That kind of distance *was* common in interactions they had experienced with other rabbis of Eric's stature. One congregant described him as "an outlier intellectually and a mensch personally." Others spoke often of him as "a brilliant but approachable teacher."

The Learner

Formative Educational Experiences

In our first interview Eric said that he felt there was nothing in his early education that would have predicted his position as a rabbi at Beth Shalom. He grew up in a traditionally observant Jewish home, attended an Orthodox school through eighth grade, and spent several hours every day after finishing classes at his public high school studying in a supplementary Orthodox school. Eric could find no indicator before his college experience that might have pointed to his current reflective approach to Jewish tradition. As a rabbi he incorporates historical, philosophical, and theological scholarship into the study of Judaism.

Nevertheless, Eric's educational biography powerfully shapes how he understands his role as a rabbinic teacher. Far more than the two other rabbis in the study, Eric's formal schooling, both Jewish and secular, emerges as a complex template that informs his philosophy and practice as a teacher. Eric was intrigued by the biographical element of my research. While initially somewhat suspicious of it, he realized its merits. In his own words:

> I think autobiography is important. I'm always very conflicted about this, by the way . . . People love, first and foremost, talking and thinking about themselves. But slightly lower than that is the interest in their leaders, right? They love rabbis talking about their lives . . . I'm not inclined to do that . . . But your biography is important to them . . . [Imagining what a congregant thinks]: *You're teaching me things.* It's important for them to know how I got to that point. What convinced me? What doubts did I have along the way? Because if they can see some of their own stuff in that, then they can say, "Maybe this is a path I can walk as well." . . . Part of being and feeling like a rabbi is not only teaching people things, but teaching them what it is to walk a certain road. It's not just the content or the substance. It's also the spiritual and intellectual process.

A prominent characteristic of Eric's educational biography centers upon his immersion in secular and Jewish studies. Eric finds ways to cogently integrate both into his worldview as a western Jew educated at elite institutions of Jewish and secular higher learning. This approach distinguishes his scholarship and his teaching. In turn, he brings the fruits of his own education into his role as a teacher of adults.

Bicultural Education

Eric's school history presents a dialectical movement between a constant dedication to Jewish learning and a stimulating absorption with secular studies. At his Orthodox Jewish elementary school, the principal in charge of general studies created a rigorous academic curriculum. Students studied everything from *Bullfinch's Mythology* to evolution. He called his learning experience there bicultural. Indeed, this descriptor set a direction for the fundamental arc of his entire academic trajectory, including time at rabbinical seminary and in graduate studies.

During college Eric underwent a pivotal transformation in his thinking about Judaism. He migrated from a traditional Orthodox outlook to a more historically driven critical understanding. Yet he remained fully committed to traditional observance. It was at this time that he began to contemplate the rabbinate. He realized that as much as he loved studying Jewish texts, being immersed in a Jewish community was equally important. While he did not see himself as a pulpit rabbi, a mentor from college steered him toward the Jewish Theological Seminary, home of the Conservative Movement's rabbinical school from which Eric received rabbinic ordination. As a first-year student, Eric approached Professor Eli Berger, an accomplished Jewish Studies scholar, ordained rabbi, and prominent leader in the American Jewish community. Eric wanted to attend graduate school in philosophy even though he was in rabbinical school. Berger wholeheartedly pushed him to do both simultaneously. Encouraged by Berger, whom Eric described as his intellectual father, he spent his four years in rabbinical school balancing rabbinic studies with analytical philosophy and logic. He received a doctorate in philosophy soon after. He seemed primed for the Ivory Tower as a scholar in academia. After graduation, he remained at the Seminary for almost two decades as a professor and administrator.

Role Models

To Eric, Berger was a brilliant academic who continued to place his vocation as a rabbinic teacher at the center of his identity and work. Berger overcame the tendency to bifurcate the mission of the scholar from that of the rabbi. Eric's work in a synagogue differs from that of his mentor, but he continues to reference Berger's model of an integrated professional identity in his current position. Crucially, Berger helped Eric learn to balance the ideological tensions inherent in adopting secular approaches to studying Judaism, derived from the nineteenth-century German model of *Wissenschaft des Judentums* (the scientific study of Judaism), with a commitment to traditional practice. In Eric's words, Berger offered a systematic and creative response to the tensions created by "refashioning tradition." To do so requires a rigorously honest confrontation with the dilemmas modernity poses to traditional interpretations of Jewish law and practice. It unabashedly incorporates such disciplines as philosophy, theology, and history. Thinking about how to adapt to the realities of the present while sustaining a dedication to traditional ritual practice guides Eric as a rabbi. It occupies a prominent place in his teaching. Eric mentioned that this approach was often "risk-filled." More laypeople were initially "frightened by it than inspired." Balancing critical thinking with traditional practice, as he espouses, requires an ability to sustain an "an open mind and a devoted heart." In Eric's case, such a challenge functions as one of the bedrock principles that inform his identity as a rabbinic teacher.

Bridging Seminary and Synagogue

Eric's two decades in academia remain important to his rabbinate. He is a respected and accomplished scholar in the fields of Jewish philosophy and theology. He continues to write. He incorporates his extensive scholarship into his congregational rabbinate through the broad array of settings in which he teaches. His position as a congregational rabbi represents a career shift, but not one as radical as his faculty colleagues viewed it when he left their circle. His academic peers expressed dismay at his decision to depart for the synagogue. Yet this choice emerged from a deepening questioning about who he aspired to be as a rabbi. When he reached his early forties, he realized that about half his life was probably behind him. He had been a rabbi in academia for eighteen years. He felt called to try something different with the next phase of his life. He decided to seek a post as a congregational rabbi. Fortuitously, Beth Shalom had begun a search for a new rabbi around the same time. It was located in a city in the same region where Eric and his family lived. It possessed an uncommon blend of progressive thinking and traditional practice. The mix was a quality that Eric found compelling. Its membership seemed to want to be challenged intellectually and as Jews by their rabbi. Beth Shalom struck him as a place where he might successfully make the transition out of full-time academia and into the congregational rabbinate.

The prospect of leading a congregation where the laity sought to deepen their knowledge and thinking about Judaism attracted Eric. It continues to be a central force in his conception of his role as a rabbinic teacher of adults. Yet, when Eric applied to Beth Shalom he suspected that his application might be received skeptically. Stereotypes about academics being disconnected from the laity abound in congregation life, according to Eric. He realized that the members might wonder about his motivation. They might be afraid that he would "speak to them in seventeen syllables" or that he would be unable to relate to them as anything other than a reserved professor.

Perhaps because he was sensitive to these biases, Eric has worked diligently to bridge the distance that customarily exists between seminary and synagogue in American Judaism. His focus on teaching and learning as a cornerstone of his rabbinate has been his guide along the way. Many congregants referred to the thoroughness of his teaching. They especially appreciated the way that he incorporated scholarly knowledge in a comprehensible and compelling manner. Learners valued how his scholarship involved more than an intellectual pursuit. Rather, they felt that teaching, learning, and writing expressed something essential about Eric's identity as a human being. Likewise, they viewed his being a congregational rabbi as much more than a professional career path. Because of this, congregants deeply valued learning with him.

Scholar in Residence

Eric described himself to me as a "scholar in residence in the community." By this he means that he consciously models his own ongoing learning for his congregants. He tries to literally embody the message that every setting in the synagogue can and even should be a place for learning. He metaphorically compared the various locales in which congregants gather in the synagogue to potential classrooms. It is important to Eric that his congregants understand that studying is very much at the heart of being a rabbi. By showing them his daily commitment to it, he seeks to reinforce that message. Furthermore, Eric hopes that when congregants see that their rabbi still has plenty to learn, they will realize that they do as well. Eric said, "I rarely talk to people about what I taught you this year. It's what we studied together this year."

Learners repeatedly referred to Eric's impressive knowledge and scholarship. But modeling his own learning is consistent with Eric's wish not to be seen as a teacher who acts only as the "dispenser of knowledge." Rather, because he continues to learn, his views about any number of subjects evolve over time. In addition to time spent with his congregant-learners, he has pursued intensive study with rabbinic colleagues through an organization that supports clergy spiritual growth. For years he has met weekly to study with a group of rabbis from each of the Jewish denominations in his city. Eric intentionally integrates the learning pursued in those environments into his teaching at Beth Shalom. He also understands the reasons why many rabbis yield to the abundant pressures of the congregational rabbinate by reducing their time for learning. But it is in the synagogue where Eric finds the most urgent need for a rabbi to keep studying. To him a congregation is the setting where he and his congregants confront theological and religious matters in their daily lives. His congregants face questions about life, death, suffering, hope, faith, and morality. Learning guides him to more competently address these issues. Eric compared a congregational rabbi's position to that of a doctor. Just as physicians must be abreast of recent medical developments to best help their patients, rabbis must keep learning in order to skillfully guide their congregants as they face the various spiritual, religious, and existential dilemmas that are part of being human.

The Value of Ideological Coherence

Eric also believes it is beneficial for his congregation to develop a measure of ideological coherence about Beth Shalom as a Jewish community. In this regard learning must lead the way. Eric's interest in ideological coherence and rational reflection points to his education as a philosopher. He incorporates this secular side of his background into his role as the synagogue's leader. By way of example, Eric described a situation early in his rabbinate at Beth Shalom. Traditionally, Jewish men are called up for the first three blessings upon reading the Torah scroll during worship based on whether they are a Cohen, Levite, or Israelite. When Eric arrived at Beth Shalom in 1994, the congregation was already gender egalitarian. Women fully participated in all aspects of prayer and study, including the Torah service.

Nevertheless, it had retained the practice of calling people to the Torah according to their status as a Cohen, Levite, or Israelite. The question of whether it was inconsistent to support gender equality but not "tribal egalitarianism" drew the attention of the ritual committee.

Eric decided that in order to arrive at a decision, he and the ritual committee needed to study the Jewish laws and the history behind the practice. During several sessions they delved into the topic using ancient, medieval, and modern texts. Together they reached a resolution that respected the custom even as they adapted it to reflect the democratic, egalitarian ideology of the congregation. The committee published its decision in the synagogue's bulletin. It is now standard practice. In Eric's analysis, studying together enabled the members of the ritual committee to achieve a reasonable consensus. They openly debated the matter as they examined its sources in Jewish tradition. They voiced different perspectives candidly. Their conclusions came after reasoning through the tensions between tradition and modernity. The solution united ritual behavior and religious ideology coherently. The implications in this approach to decision-making are far-reaching for how building consensus through learning shapes communal identity at Beth Shalom.

In spite of Eric's emphasis on learning, he acknowledged that he had never taken a course in educational theory or adult education. He bases his ideas about teaching and learning on practical experience. The "apprenticeship of observation" (Lortie 1975) with his own teachers throughout the years also affects his ideas. As an extension of this admission, Eric spoke candidly about one of the main challenges of the congregational rabbinate: finding time for sustained philosophical or theoretical reflection. He distinguished this kind of learning from the studying he does on a day-to-day basis. The time needed to refresh one's ideas is often lacking in the rabbinate. In fact, Eric, like Jonathan Fisk, noted that our interviews represented an unusual opportunity for him to step back and give himself time to muse out loud about teaching, learning, and his role as a rabbinic teacher.

ERIC'S COURSES

Beth Shalom provides numerous adult education courses and programs for its members. This programmatic richness is consistent with the leadership of a senior rabbi who puts teaching and learning at the center of his rabbinate. All three rabbis on the staff teach adults on a weekly basis. Other Jewish educators on Beth Shalom's staff also offer classes for adults. Eric teaches many different courses on a weekly or biweekly basis. Although he and his rabbinic colleagues teach mini-courses throughout the year, I focused on the ongoing classes. During my time at Beth Shalom I observed Eric teaching adults in the following classes:

- A weekly, Shabbat morning seminar-style theology study circle that meets for one hour before services in the synagogue's foyer. Learners sit on the sofa and in chairs placed around a coffee table. Approximately a dozen adults attend, primarily in their forties and fifties, the majority of whom are men.

- A weekly Jewish literature lecture/question-answer class that focuses primarily on the Bible. It meets in the late morning for an hour and a half in one of the large social halls. Food and beverages are available for the attendees. The learners sit at large rectangular tables. Approximately fifty adults attend, primarily ranging in age from their sixties to eighties, the majority of whom are women.

- A weekly Hebrew reading class that meets for one hour in the small sanctuary on Sunday morning. The learners read from a learner's Hebrew language newspaper to practice developing the reading and translation skills of contemporary Hebrew. Approximately ten people attend, with a balance between men and women.

- A biweekly Mishnah (Oral Law) class that meets on Tuesday evenings for two hours in the synagogue's library. The attendees sit with the rabbi around a long rectangular table and in additional chairs set up around the perimeter of the table. Approximately thirty people attend, with a fairly even balance between men and women.

- A biweekly Talmud (Oral Law) class for congregants that meets offsite during the week at lunchtime in the metropolitan offices of one of the members. This class enables professionals who work long hours to study Talmud with the rabbi.

These classes have existed for at least a decade. The Talmud class predates Eric's arrival at Beth Shalom. In addition, a substantial number of the learners in each of the classes have been studying with Eric and with each other for a sustained period of time. The learners and Eric decide together their choice of topics and texts. Textual analysis plays a central part in all the courses. Texts always include an English translation.

THEMES IN ERIC'S TEACHING PRACTICE

Integrating Intellectual and Spiritual Concerns

As a rabbi and philosopher who spent his first decades in a seminary, Eric knows that his natural intellectual bent can dominate his rabbinate. Evidently, Eric is comfortable with conceptualizing education as a process of inquiry, analysis, and synthesis, similar to how scholars in academia teach and study. Since becoming a congregational rabbi, however, he has discovered that this approach too easily excludes or overlooks the spiritual needs of his learners. Increasingly, he found that it stymied his own spiritual growth. Getting to know his congregants as individuals over the span of many years and interacting with them about matters from the mundane to the profound has sensitized Eric to reflect upon spiritual concerns. He does so to a much greater extent than he did with seminary students.

Eric understands spirituality in broad terms. It concerns human beings recognizing that they are part of something greater than themselves—whether that is a transcendent God, an immanent God, some general force at work in the universe, or inside their own hearts and minds. The main point is to accept that human beings are not the be-all and end-all of existence. Eric finds that in our society a focus on personal success and on feeding our egos is rewarded rather than restrained. In his prosperous community of ambitious households, remembering that living involves much more than the external markers of wealth and status requires daily effort. Awareness can get buried. Part of his role as a religious leader and teacher is to avoid being overwhelmed personally by such powerful social messages. It is also to invite his congregants to see the world differently.

In the course of our discussion about the balance between the intellectual and the spiritual, I asked Eric to talk about what he understood by the phrase, "Teaching Torah." He did not rush to provide an answer. When he began to speak, there were unusually long pauses as he searched for the accurate words. He prefaced his remarks by clarifying that Torah for him did not refer exclusively to the corpus of sacred Jewish writings. He specified emphatically that he did not teach Torah from an exclusivist perspective. He did not view Jewish tradition as intrinsically superior to other religious traditions:

> Torah to me is anything that forces you to confront, be in contact with, puts you in touch with the deeper meaning of why we're here. . . . Teaching Torah at its best is modeling and empowering people

to extract that kind of meaning from their own tradition and to use auxiliary traditions to enlighten it. That's how I try to teach.

This orientation toward Torah runs steadily throughout Eric's teaching. It makes him sensitive to and wary of overt or covert expressions of innate Jewish superiority on the part of his learners and his colleagues. It gives him the freedom to expose adult learners in a Conservative synagogue to what he views as the universalistic, redemptive purposes of religious law. It is a daunting task.

Role Modeling a Spiritual Search

Part of Eric's evolution as a congregational rabbi includes an ever-deepening responsiveness to spirituality as a lived practice rather than a theoretical construct. He said that his colleagues in academia often find it astonishing that he describes the day-to-day responsibilities of working in a synagogue as spiritual. Yet, in Eric's experience, participating in ritual events and liminal moments in people's lives compels him to ask questions that he did not pose as a professor. As a result, several years ago Eric enrolled in a program sponsored by an organization that works with rabbis, cantors, and Jewish educators on Jewish spirituality. For eighteen months he met with a cohort. During retreats and regular meetings he immersed himself in exploring Jewish spirituality. Doing so helped him clarify how his images of God affect his personal life and his identity as a rabbi. He continues to attend events sponsored by the organization. During one of my observations he told his learners that he would be away and out of communication for a week on a silent retreat.

Out of his own immersion, Eric developed more confidence in raising the subject of God and spirituality with his congregants. Just as he has come to feel more strongly that "exploring the spiritual side of human life, human nature, is an important part of what it means to be a Jew," so, too, does he want to be a guide for his congregants in these matters. In 2007 Eric spearheaded the creation of a monthly Shabbat contemplative service. At the time of my research, approximately fifty people attended. Part of the service includes meditating silently and singing Hasidic melodies. Another important component includes text study. The group studies Hasidic texts as a means of generating images of God. The sources chosen encourage congregants to contemplate how spiritual concerns and their images of God affect them.

The service has been a positive learning opportunity for Eric, too. He admitted that while he likes the metaphor of his rabbinate as a classroom, it also risks leading him to be overly intellectual in his orientation. He has become more sensitive to the inadvertent negative messages that such a metaphor can evoke for congregants. He does not want them to see him as a rabbi who cares only about ideas. Over the years he has come to feel more strongly that addressing their spiritual lives is fundamental to his teaching and to who he is as a rabbi.

In the contemplative service teaching Torah includes an explicit focus on spiritual concerns. Although most congregants do not attend and, therefore, do not learn with him in that setting, it nonetheless has a broader influence. Congregants are aware that spirituality matters to Eric as their rabbi. They are not surprised when he introduces its themes into other educational settings. Teaching Torah to him means consciously striving to be aware of the intellectual and the spiritual dimensions of Jewish learning. His perseverance in this regard conveys to his learners a seriousness of commitment to the process. It models a determination to move beyond his natural comfort zone as he works on his spiritual development. Throughout, his behaviors signal to the adults that as their rabbi he is most certainly their devoted teacher, but he remains a dedicated learner.

A Facilitator of Learning

Toward the end of my final interview with Eric, he pointed to a small frame hanging on one of the walls in his office. In elegant Hebrew calligraphy inside the frame were the famous words from the first chapter of *Ethics of the Fathers* (*m.* 6): "Provide yourself with a teacher and get yourself a [student] companion." Eric mentioned that a group of graduating high school seniors gave it to him as a gift. It meant a great deal to him because it suggested that his teenage students saw him as their rabbi and their friend. Eric's interpretation hints at a quality he strives for in his teaching practice that is best described as facilitating learning.

In his answer to an e-mail message I wrote, Eric gave a thoughtful response outlining his own sense of the term "facilitating":

> I do see it as my job to share knowledge and also share questions and perplexities at the same time—to leave people with a sense of an open-textured tradition. I think it is not only more respectful of them as learners, but also more true to the nature of the

tradition as well... That doesn't mean that I don't have to transmit to them things I know that they don't, but I try to make it clear that whereas I know some things they don't in some areas, that's a relatively minor gap compared to what we still have to learn together.

Facilitating is a way of conceptualizing teaching that emphasizes shared exploration. As a facilitator, Eric orients the teaching toward the learning process rather than toward coverage of any predetermined subject matter. Symbolically and literally, Eric joins the learners at the table. Indeed, in two of the classes that Eric teaches on a regular basis, the Shabbat morning theology study and the Tuesday evening Mishnah class, he sits with his learners. The Shabbat class meets in an informal circle around a coffee table in the entryway to the synagogue, while the Mishnah class gathers at a large table in the synagogue's library. As a facilitator, Eric listens carefully. He provides ample opportunities for the learners to interact directly with each other instead of having all their comments addressed to him as the expert. He presents himself as a co-learner with them in their educational journey.

Modeling a Thinking Process

Eric's description of himself as a facilitator emphasizes the idea of being a learner among learners. This role includes modeling a thinking process as an integral part of studying any topic. Eric hopes to initiate his learners into a process for exploring the meaning in a given text or topic. The purpose is to help "generate understanding," a learning outcome that Eric referred to as one of his teaching aims.

Generating understanding far exceeds accumulating factual knowledge. Rather, it involves being able first to assimilate new information. In turn, learners must be prepared to analyze and synthesize the information so that it becomes knowledge. Eventually, the knowledge transforms into new understandings about how to live. Eric referred to Socrates's comparison of the role of the teacher to that of a midwife in this context. His assessment of Socrates's metaphor suggests that learning often includes a certain measure of "struggling" and "discomfort." The stakes are high. The outcomes are not foregone conclusions. The teacher as midwife is present to "enable something to come forth safely..." in Eric's words. Success happens when "something whole and viable comes out... even if it doesn't look like you." Eric's metaphorical comparison of his role to that of Socrates's teacher-as-midwife implies that facilitating inevitably requires a degree of risk-taking.

My observations of Eric's teaching helped contextualize the metaphor. The educational exchanges in Eric's classes involve a willingness to pose difficult questions about Judaism. He expects learners to face the complexity and the contradictions in Jewish tradition. The discussions require that the teacher and learner listen respectfully to divergent perspectives and interpretations. The participants embrace the idea that learning influences and transforms them in unanticipated ways. They acknowledge that understandings about the meaning of one's life and the nature of one's commitments as a Jewish human being may be altered. The conversations challenge teacher and learners to incorporate new perceptions in a manner that supports rather than undermines a dedication to living a Jewish life.

Eric, as the teacher who facilitates this process, accepts responsibility for accompanying the learners throughout. Just as when a midwife stays with the woman who is in labor, the supportive nature of his facilitator orientation matters to Eric. The learners need to trust that the facilitator will be present for them as they journey through the thinking process. It also suggests that the teacher-learner relationship includes an element of disparity. The teacher as midwife possesses an expertise that the learner as laboring woman depends upon. Although they experience the process together, the dynamic is an inherently unequal one. The learners are active participants, but they are also vulnerable. They need the teacher's support to see them through safely.

To assure learners that he is fulfilling those responsibilities, Eric presents them with a predictable structure. He asks open-ended questions when initiating a new topic of study. He revisits these queries during the course of the learning. He presents coherent arguments from multiple perspectives about the topic. Through discussion he and his learners reflect upon the validity of the arguments and ideas. He draws on Jewish and non-Jewish sources to consider possible conclusions. The emphasis on such a thinking process finds its solid roots in Eric's own educational history. To facilitate means to help learners achieve a level of intellectual sophistication regarding Judaism. Eric sets the learning bar high for his adult learners.

Discussion as a Teaching Aim of Facilitation

The back and forth of discussion is one reason why Eric favors facilitation. Eric cited several specific recent examples that had reinforced for him the beneficial dialogue that discussion sustains. He mentioned political events and divorce law as complex issues that recently emerged during different courses. What he especially relished was how out of discussion new insights and ideas germinate. The decision to employ discussion as a facilitation tool reflects Eric's openness towards his learners' experiences, views, and questions. This is true regardless of their background knowledge. Even when he teaches a topic about which he possesses strong beliefs and convictions, through discussion Eric models an open-ended, inquiry-based approach to learning.

In turn, the learners take their cues from Eric. They discover that in discussion they will reach their own conclusions. These may or may not coincide with those of their rabbi. The assumptions they initially brought to the topic may require reevaluation. According to one middle-aged congregant who had been studying with Eric for eight years at the time of the research, "He is intellectually curious, passionate, has a wide reach, but is not dogmatic. He is not there to tell you what to think." Or, as a learner who had been studying with Eric for a few years succinctly remarked, "He throws it out and lets it come back. He doesn't have an agenda to settle."

Obstacles to Facilitation

Settings do exist, however, that challenge Eric's intentions. In particular, a group with more than thirty people is a potential stumbling block. Eric is aware of the changed dynamic in larger groups. Yet in the interviews he pointed out that during Shabbat morning services, when as many as three hundred worshippers may attend, he still generally prefers to "teach" rather than "preach" from the pulpit. By this he means that he prefers to facilitate text study. He is happiest transforming the sanctuary into an interactive learning environment in which the congregants study sources and respond to him and each other.

Eric offered several examples of recent Shabbat services during which he engaged in such teaching. He mentioned two international events—one that affected the Jewish world and Israel directly and one that did not—where he believed the moral issues warranted closer attention through the lens of Jewish textual sources and Jewish law. Eric described how he proceeded to use either an event or a text as a starting point. Rather than leave the learners with a final word of wisdom, he made a point to finish with a question for them to keep pondering. Eric said that even though his own teaching goals with a large group and a small group are not fundamentally different, he knows that in a large group there is less opportunity for him to listen, and much less of a chance for discussion. Large groups create an imbalance because the teacher risks becoming a lecturer or a performer. Facilitation, in contrast, requires a higher degree of symmetrical interactions. In larger groups, such symmetry is improbable if not impossible.

As a result, Eric realizes that in a large group his goal of generating understanding through facilitation does not work as successfully as it does in more intimate settings. In the smaller groups that meet regularly, in which Eric has the opportunity to know his learners better, the weekly meetings and the frequent verbal interactions make it possible to identify whether his facilitation does indeed "generate understanding." In larger groups, Eric does not yet seem to have other mechanisms in place to determine the extent to which his goal of generating understanding is being achieved. If he were to clarify for himself those settings and subjects that lend themselves either to facilitation or to more frontal teaching, he may be able to create an even greater coherence in his teaching style than already exists.

A Trustworthy Guide

While being a facilitator is Eric's preferred approach as a teacher, he also brings a different style and accompanying set of practices to his teaching. It is not lecture-oriented but is qualitatively different from facilitation. It is best described through the image of a trustworthy guide. Eric clearly treasures unearthing the complexity of the subjects he teaches. He has the intellectual acumen to do so quite skillfully. He has a devoted group of adult learners in the congregation who want to learn with him precisely because of his lively intelligence and thorough scholarship. As a result, in certain learning situations Eric directs the learners purposefully through subjects and texts as an authoritative expert.

Succeeding in this approach without projecting the image of a brilliant but distant scholar represents one of Eric's teaching strengths as a rabbi. He employs several strategies to avoid creating a hierarchical learning environment for the adults even when he teaches this way. These strategies include adding humor, respecting all questions, offering anecdotal stories that relate to the theme or topic in a way that involve people's lived experiences (including his own), and translating difficult texts (whether from Hebrew to English, or from abstruse scholarly language in English into colloquial language) in a way that links the subject to learners' prior knowledge. As a guide Eric describes himself as "someone who takes you through a certain forbidding terrain, and reminds you that you can actually get through this . . . I know something about this. That doesn't mean you don't have to put in some effort. But you don't have to be seized with anxiety about failure or danger." For Eric, reliable guides ensure that wherever learners go with them, they will be safe and sound along the way.

In this context, Eric mentioned a recent meeting with lay leaders from his synagogue. The members, whom he called facilitators, were spearheading study groups with congregants as part of a broader initiative to stimulate Conservative congregations to think more reflectively about the idea of mitzvah, often translated as "commandment." Eric grew very animated when he described what took place:

> Last evening I had a meeting with the facilitators who had lots of feedback for me, and lots of questions, and doubts about where we are going. In the course of this meeting I was doing a number of things. I was explicating to them certain things—What's the next unit coming up? Why is this text chosen? Why are they [the people attending the various sessions] asking these questions? What's the import of them? How can you [as facilitators] be answering some of these questions for yourselves and also trying to bring out the answers that are latent in the hearts and the minds of the people in your group?
>
> I'm giving them a sense of confidence that you don't have to have all the answers. You're of this group, you're not over the group, but you're there to help these important ideas emerge, in which there is no right answer, but there is an authenticity of the conversation and in the struggle of ideas. My comments were very helpful to them. They were kind of reenergized in lots of ways. I can say that I felt very much like a rabbi. I wasn't standing up there in the old mode of saying, "Here's the wisdom I'm dispensing to you." I was doing what I felt I really got into this to do—empowering people to believe in—what's the word here?—the trueness of their questioning.

The "trueness of their questioning" describes the authenticity that Eric strives for as a guide. Seen from this perspective, the adults who learn regularly with Eric develop their own teaching abilities. These learners have the potential to become a cadre of lay Jewish educators within the heart of the synagogue. In fact, there was evidence of such a development in the Shabbat morning theology group. Several years ago Eric proposed that the group coordinate and lead the teaching for the all-night study sessions held on Shavuot, the late spring holiday that celebrates the revelation of the Torah and the Ten Commandments, as narrated in the Book of Exodus. The success of that initial endeavor continues into the present. Before Shavuot the learner-congregants as teachers gather for dinner at Eric's home. They plan the program with him. They choose the themes and the texts, which they in turn teach. Eric guides them toward becoming "in-house teachers" of Torah during the holiday.

As a trustworthy guide Eric mentors his learners on their journey. Mentorship has a long and rich history in Jewish education. Descriptions of it abound in the Talmud regarding the relations between sages and students (Aberbach 1967). Mentorship also occupies an important place in adult learning scholarship. In his research on mentors in adult education, author Laurent Daloz found a complex web of connections joining mentoring, adult learning, and adult development. He turned to the metaphor of a journey in his analysis of a student's evolution and a mentor's role. He observed: "Like guides, we walk at times ahead of our students, at times beside them; at times, we follow their lead. In sensing where to walk lies our art, for as we support our students in their struggle, challenge them toward their best, and cast light on the road ahead, we do so in the name of our respect for their potential and our care for their growth" (1999, 244). In this description, Daloz pinpoints a process that Eric embraces as a rabbinic educator. It links Eric's sincere regard for every person's potential to learn with his awareness of the penetratingly spiritual aspects of Torah study. It more than hints at the way that a relationship between a teacher and a learner helps us, in Eric's words, to be "in touch with why we are really here."

THE LEARNING CONGREGATION

As a congregational rabbi, Eric's role exemplifies Rina Lewin's description of a "teaching rabbinate." In a teaching rabbinate, education is at the center of congregational life. Adults become acculturated to the idea that learning is a key, and may be the key to who they are as Jews. Learning acts as a motivating reason for belonging to the synagogue and for remaining actively involved in its daily rhythms. Eric leads the way by modeling a teaching style that exemplifies his own dedication to learning. He inspires congregants to deepen their understanding of Judaism through facilitating and guiding, rather than lecturing or preaching. Learning becomes the map by which congregants navigate the complexity of Jewish tradition in their own lives.

Jewish education also functions as the activity that creates ideological coherence in the synagogue. It supports the creation of multiple learning cohorts through which long-term study on a regular basis develops knowledgeable Jews. Eric models the ways that his learners can find in Judaism responses to the deepest questions human beings face about their existence. As a teacher of adults, Eric's ability to keep, in his own words, "an open mind and a devoted heart" serves as an example for his adult learners of what is possible. Together, they explore the depth and dynamism of Judaism. Together, they reinvigorate the well-trod thoroughfares of Jewish tradition, creating along the way new pathways of discovery for themselves and for future generations.

chapter 5

RABBIS AS FACILITATORS

Jonathan, Rina, and Eric articulate an egalitarian, anti-hierarchical vision of themselves as teachers. They embrace their adult learners' right to be fully respected as learners regardless of the depth or kind of Jewish content knowledge they may lack as adults. They also strive to help their learners gain new levels of Jewish insight, perspective, and engagement. Achieving these kinds of knowledge is far more important than acquiring only the basics of textual or ritual competency. Rather, it calls for intrapersonal and interpersonal growth in one's connections to Judaism. In this kind of a learning experience, all three rabbis view themselves as facilitators.

Yet we must use this term carefully. Given the extent to which rabbis can exert even an unintended influence on their learner-congregants by virtue of their clergy identity, the rabbi-as-facilitator treads on potentially fragile terrain, at least initially. What are the qualities demonstrated by rabbis when they strive to relate to their learners as facilitators? How do they integrate the reality of their leadership, influence, and authority as rabbis of the congregation with their belief in the democratic spirit expressed by being facilitators of learning?

As chapter 1 indicates, many influential theories of adult learning highlight facilitation as a key component of teaching adults. As a concept, facilitation includes a diversity of understandings. These range, for example, from andragogy's focus on support, to transformational learning theory's emphasis on guided critical reflection. As Stephen Brookfield (2006) and Patricia Cranton (2006) affirmed, facilitation requires a subtle and sophisticated blend of authenticity and credibility. In her work on adult Jewish learning, Diane Schuster also addressed the importance of authenticity and credibility (2003). Credibility generally refers to the educator's content expertise and authenticity to the interpersonal rapport with learners. Even so, these qualities defy compact definitions. But there is general agreement that in relation to the adult educator, the two concepts are essential to successful teaching (Brookfield 2006). The following discussion includes an analysis of them in light of rabbis as facilitators.

PRECONCEIVED IMAGES OF RABBIS

How rabbis endeavor to judiciously balance content expertise and interpersonal authenticity offers additional insight into the inherently complex dimensions of teaching as facilitation. When rabbis adopt their facilitator role, they may initially generate discomfort in their adult learners because congregants often relate to rabbis as authority figures. Interacting with their clergy as facilitators may call for a fundamental shift in their relationship with them. How to attend to this discomfort and channel it toward constructive rather than destructive ends requires a particularly keen social-emotional skill set.

Many adults remain primed for the rabbi-as-preacher or the rabbi-as-lecturer when they venture into adult learning. This expectation, according to Brookfield, is to be anticipated because adults often return to the dependent attitude they acquired as younger learners in educational settings (1986, 136). As a result of this dynamic, rabbis need to show sensitivity as they acclimate their adult learners to a potentially new way of relating to them. The rabbis have to help the adults turn their focus away from the rabbi-as-expert and toward the learner-as-seeker. It is precisely through this realignment of the rabbi-adult learner relationship that the excitement generated by deeper adult forms of learning begins to take shape.

Approachability

Approachability as an interpersonal stance is essential to successful rabbinic facilitation with adults. Approachability reinforces the egalitarian tone that the rabbis set. As rabbis, Jonathan, Rina, and Eric are conscious of the heavy symbolic power attached to the clergy title and position. Two of the three rabbis referred to rabbi and clinical psychologist Jack Bloom's (1976) description of the rabbi as a symbolic exemplar. They conceded that they grasped the distance that such a position can create. Yet precisely because of that awareness, they seek to overcome this gap when they teach. In other words, they self-consciously wear their symbolic exemplarhood lightly. Through such approachability they strive for a greater symmetry between themselves and their learners.

The rabbis manifest this approachability in a variety of ways. These include: being on a first-name basis with their learners; generally dressing casually rather than formally when teaching; sharing information about their private lives within appropriate personal boundaries; inviting learners to gather for study in settings outside of the synagogue, such as in congregants' homes, offices, clubs, on retreats, and in the rabbis' homes; and accepting invitations to meet with the learners outside of the synagogue in certain instances. The latter might include attending a synagogue event organized by laity but held in a private location, such as a member's home or at a restaurant. They thereby support learning in a variety of informal social contexts. By gathering outside the synagogue itself, both the rabbi and the learners encounter each other in environments where they are less constrained by the formal atmosphere generated by an institutional space. Finally, but crucially, the rabbis make themselves approachable by carefully refraining from prescriptive or judgmental verbal remarks towards their learners' levels of Jewish knowledge or observance.

A logical rationale animates these efforts, driven by two insights expressed by all of the rabbis. The first is that their adult learners often bring a history of modest or ambivalent memories associated with Jewish education and synagogues. A second is that their adult learners require developmentally appropriate interactions with their rabbi. According to Brookfield, adult learners frequently express a "feeling of being undeserving imposters who will sooner or later have their real, pathetically inadequate identities revealed" (1991, 40). His observation holds accurate for rabbi-adult learner relationships. In her 2003 book and in her article "Teaching Jewish Adults" Schuster found that adult Jewish learners often feel vulnerable about their lack of Jewish knowledge. They frequently bring memories of negative Jewish learning experiences and encounters with rabbis (2003).

Several anecdotes (also included in the portraits) strikingly illuminate each of the rabbi's efforts in this area. When Rina summed up a description of her family history to a large group of religious school parents by saying, "I tell you all this because I don't want you to think that my family is any different from yours," she invited the attendees to start seeing her as a "normal" person, rather than a perfect role model. When Jonathan discussed the influence of his non-Jewish stepfather on his Jewish development in one of his High Holiday sermons, he signaled to the congregation that being part of a mixed-religion family was not something out of the ordinary, even for a rabbi. On the contrary, a caring and supportive non-Jewish parental figure led him to further connection with Jewish tradition. By speaking from personal experience he sought to remove the stigma that some of his congregants may feel around the subject. Finally, in one of our interviews Eric explained how during a brief but worrisome episode of hearing loss, he decided to share his response to the illness with his congregants rather than minimizing or concealing it. He consciously chose to share his fears and vulnerability about his mortality in response to being sick. These three examples highlight the ways that, the rabbis try to "stand among the congregants rather than on a pulpit above them" (Wertheimer 2005, 44). This approachability creates an atmosphere in which rabbinic facilitation can thrive rather than be stymied.

Moderating Discussion

On its own, however, approachability does not suffice for successful facilitation. It prepares the terrain for a particular kind of social-emotional interaction that informs the rabbis' teaching. Much of education involves talking. Consequently, the nature of talking warrants attention; in particular, how discussion shapes the teaching-learning exchange with adults. Definitions of discussion abound in the adult education literature. They often overlap with such terms as "conversation" and "dialogue." Researchers use similar terminology to refer to different aspects of "group talk." Stephen Brookfield and Stephen Preskill offer a definition that is close to the results of my research:

> In general we define discussion as an alternately serious and playful effort by a group of two or more to share views and engage in mutual and reciprocal critique. The purposes of discussion are fourfold: (1) to help participants reach a more critically informed understanding about the topic or topics under consideration, (2) to enhance participants' self-awareness and their capacity for self-critique, (3) to foster an appreciation among participants for the diversity of opinion that invariably emerges when viewpoints are exchanged openly and honestly, and (4) to act as a catalyst to helping people take informed action in the world (2005, 4).

It is through this approach to discussion that the adults in our rabbis' congregations expose their questions, ideas, beliefs, and perspectives. They develop the ability to critique and reflect upon their own thinking and that of their fellow learners. They are challenged to hear other points of view that may transform their own. Jonathan, Rina, and Eric structure their study groups so that discussion drives learning. Discussion helps the participants get to know each other's views, rather than hearing only the rabbi's perspective. Discussion sustains active participation on the part of the learners. It allows questions and concerns to emerge organically. It also democratizes the learning setting. The learners discover the legitimacy and validity of their perspectives, not only of the rabbis' or of Jewish tradition.

Through discussion the rabbis create an ambience whereby the adults will engage with each other instead of directing all talk to the rabbi as the expert. The rabbis work diligently to avoid dominating the conversation verbally. In the small- and medium-sized groups, the back and forth of discussion among learners takes precedence over any other kind of exchange. In larger groups all three make determined efforts to encourage interactive discussion. This is the case even when it would be easier, and certainly more efficient in regard to coverage of material, to move to a lecture or question-and-answer format.

Facilitating a discussion, however, is different from participating in an informal conversation. Facilitation requires preparation even though Brookfield and Preskill pointed out the paradox in attempting to pre-plan an open discussion (2005). In this regard, the rabbis show flexibility by their willingness to allow the learners' concerns and queries to shape the discussion. They also exhibit the capacity to redirect it when necessary. Finding the proper balance requires advance devising by the rabbis. At other times, even when the rabbis have put together a discussion topic, the direction of the conversation subsequently leads away from their initial agenda. Yet in interviews and e-mail exchanges that followed my observations, none of the rabbis found the potentially unpredictable or unwieldy discussion climate threatening. Rather, they accepted its serendipitous nature as part of facilitation.

Their willingness to let the learners frequently lead the way presupposes a trust on the part of the rabbis toward them. This quality is not to be underestimated. Trust builds an emotional and ethical relationship of transformative significance between the rabbis and the learners. The description of discussion by Brookfield and Preskill (offered above) accentuates the intellectually stimulating aspect of learning while paying less attention to the affective dimensions. Trusting in the learners' capacities to sustain discussion turns facilitation into an embodiment of confidence, faith, and respect. The implicit message conveyed through such trust hinges on the essential dignity of their learners. It reveals the rabbis' profoundly spiritual and moral stance toward the adults they teach. To facilitate in this manner reveals the sacredness of interpersonal relationships as they are expressed through verbal discourse.

Generating Open-Ended Questions

As facilitators of learning, rabbis also model this trust through their approach to questions. They do not want to control the kinds of questions their learners ask. Neither do the rabbis want to give prepared answers to queries they present to the learners. Rather, they favor open-ended exploration. Open-ended questions refer to those inquiries that do not have immediately obvious correct or incorrect answers. Jerold Apps asserted that open-ended questions were a key factor in developing higher-level thinking skills among adults (1991). Educational psychologists Irving Sigel, Jeffrey Kress, and Maurice Elias, who root their research in cognitive-developmental theories, argued that Jewish educators who employed intentional questioning strategies, including open-ended questions, aided Jewish identity development (2007). The authors' analysis of questioning strategies correlates to findings from my research. Open-ended questioning strategies serve affective and cognitive purposes. These include:

- Incorporating the learners' affective experiences into any topic of study (55–56).
- Challenging the learners to make cognitive connections between their prior knowledge and the topic of study (59).

These elements form part of facilitating a learning process that helps adults in two valuable ways: by providing multiple entry points into studying Jewish texts, topics, and concepts; and by inviting creativity rather than rigidity in response to the material (Sigel et al. 2007, 62–63). The key premise underlying the rabbis' questioning methods is that the learners can arrive at their own answers to these questions. Asking open-ended questions is integral to what Eric and Jonathan mean when they speak about "teaching not preaching" as rabbinic educators. Part of the "teach, don't preach" dynamic includes framing a topic with questions that lead the learners to draw their own conclusions. It is also part of Rina's emphasis on multiple religious "truths" rather than one monolithic truth. To acknowledge that no one person or system can ever claim possession of the only right answer to any religious subject drives Rina's ability to model for her learners the value of open-ended questions.

GUIDING LEARNING AS AN EXPERT

By now you may be wondering where the rabbi's own many years of immersion in Jewish text study fit into this schema. Perhaps you are asking, "Can't anyone be a facilitator? Why is being a rabbi so important?" While it is true that the facilitation skills described here are transferable to adult educators other than rabbis, there are indeed aspects of facilitation as a clergy educator that are distinctive. In this section I address facilitation as a way of guiding that brings the expert knowledge of sacred texts and rituals possessed by clergy into conversation with their teaching practice. Midwifery and journeys are two evocative metaphors that present compelling images of rabbis as teachers who authoritatively guide their learners even as they remain facilitators.

Midwifery

Rina and Eric independently referred to midwives in conceptualizing themselves as teachers (see chapters 3 and 4). To Rina, the image of a midwife suggests facilitating the growth of intrapersonal connections to Judaism for the individual learner via the educational process. It also means supporting the development of interpersonal bonds through Jewish learning. She includes in this context both the relationships among fellow learners and within the larger body of her congregation. For Eric, the image captures the excitement and the risk at the core of his purpose as a rabbinic teacher. For both rabbis, the midwife metaphor reflects their self-perception as caring, helpful, skillful, and knowledgeable expert guides.

As such, teaching becomes a collaborative endeavor that holds creative promise and potential perils. Mary Field Belenky and her colleagues put the teacher as midwife image at the center of their feminist description and analysis of connected teaching with adult female learners (1986). It serves us well for our rabbis:

> Midwife-teachers focus not on their own knowledge (as the lecturer does) but on the students' knowledge. They contribute when

needed, but it is always clear that the baby is not theirs but the student's... The connected teacher tries to create groups in which members can nurture each other's thoughts to maturity (1986, 218–21).

In Plato's *Theaetetus,* Socrates elaborated on the idea of the role of the teacher as midwife in language that parallels the description offered by Belenky and her colleagues. In both, the focus turns to helping the learner give birth to wisdom and understanding. The midwife metaphor, as a consequence, implies that teachers bring a level of expertise and experience to their role. What transpires in the teacher-learner encounter includes elements of the unwieldy and unpredictable; the encounter can be a potentially difficult and transformative process for the learner. To see oneself as a midwife also implies that the rabbi will likely be stretched in unanticipated ways, albeit differently than the learner. To extend the metaphor, it suggests that as facilitators, rabbis must constantly renew their knowledge of the subject and their familiarity with their learners. Their learners undergo a labor process that is painful at times. Still, both parties bring the hope and expectation of a fulfilling outcome.

Once again, the theme of trust enters into the conception of the rabbi as facilitator through this metaphor. The learners must feel confidence in their rabbi's accumulated knowledge and wisdom. They also must feel assured that the rabbi will accompany them through any struggles. Both parties become vulnerable if serious difficulties arise. For example, Rina's difficulties with her adult B'nei Mitzvah class provided an opportunity for me to witness her vulnerability. She sensed that something was awry in the group's dynamic. It troubled her. Her response was to reach out to them honestly. To resolve the problems she included the learners, frankly encouraging them to be open with each other and with her. While what she heard upset her, it also engendered the possibility for redirection and improvement with her supportive guidance. As a group they worked through the process together.

Eric offered a different kind of example, albeit one with similar overtones. He shared that he had encountered a learner who resisted his approach to Jewish learning. Eric described his efforts over the course of various one-on-one conversations with the learner to be honest about his understanding of teaching and learning and to listen to the man's needs. They mutually reached an awareness that it would be wiser for the congregant to seek out a different kind of rabbinic teacher rather than remain frustrated and stymied in his studying with Eric.

Journeys

Eric proposed a second guiding metaphor during one of our interviews. In addition to speaking about the teacher as midwife, he referred to learning in general and to Jewish text study in particular as a journey. The voyage Eric described is not meant to be easy. If it were, a guide would be unnecessary. Instead, it evoked a wilderness experience. There are challenges to encounter. They are not insurmountable, but they do require effort. The rabbi, as guide, accompanies the learners to ensure that they will not get lost on the way.

Eric is not unique in this choice of metaphor. Schuster compared adult Jewish learning to a journey. She linked it to adult identity development. In *Jewish Lives, Jewish Learning*, she showed how over the course of a learning journey, adult Jews look to their teachers as resourceful, supportive guides (2003, 61–79). Laurent Daloz also chose the metaphor of a journey to conceptualize the process of adult learning in his book *Mentor: Guiding the Journey of Adult Learning* (1999). In his case, the setting was higher education. For him, the adult educator leads the learners through a journey as their mentor. In an interview many years earlier he had described the mentors who facilitate this process as guiding a soul journey: "In a certain sense, the deep understanding of mentorship finds us dropping back to that level where we are talking about a role or work that involves shepherding the soul" (Peruniak 1990).

In their distinctive contexts Schuster and Daloz identified the necessity for the adult educator as facilitator to give careful attention to processes and relationships. These aspects of being a guide include a particularly complex blend of skills and dispositions. They encompass: knowledge of subject matter and its possible implications for the learners; familiarity with the strengths and weaknesses of the learners; an awareness of the direction that learners need to move toward, although not a rigidly defined path or map; and an appreciation of the individual learner's readiness to embark on the journey.

Guiding Text Study

Text study is one prominent area in which the rabbis often invoke their guide role. The three rabbis use a variety of classical Jewish texts and sometimes non-Jewish ones from a variety of eras in their teaching. All three include the Tanakh (Hebrew Bible) as an ongoing subject. They also incorporate modern and contemporary Jewish literature in their teaching. Books by such authors as Anita Diamant and Abraham Joshua Heschel, among others, are regularly incorporated in their teaching.

Nevertheless, Jewish text study can be a daunting prospect for adult Jews, even those with prior Jewish education of varying levels. The ancient sources initially seem very distant from their contemporary lives. The knowledge that the original language (Hebrew or Aramaic) is not their own can intimidate them. The learners bring memories of childhood exposure that too often bored or alienated them from these crucibles of Jewish tradition.

To the rabbis it is essential to help learners face these anxieties, as well as any others that surface over the course of text study. Guiding text study ushers adult learners into an interpretive process in their encounter with the Jewish canon. It is a collaborative endeavor that includes intellectual and emotional components. The rabbis do this by first establishing a climate that values and validates the learner's level of ability, knowledge, and questions. They assure the participants that feelings of competence and insight are achievable. Based on my observations, such a message is underscored by Rina's insistence that no question is a stupid question, by Jonathan's assurances that all sources include an English translation, and by Eric's incorporation of non-Jewish sources as a basis for comparison with Jewish ones. When questions arise during text study to which the rabbis do not have immediate answers, they willingly acknowledge their own limitations. Their credibility is based on expert knowledge that is buttressed by the studying and thinking they do along with their learners and with their rabbinic colleagues.

The rabbis ground their credibility as guides in solid and deep knowledge of the material they teach. They display a similar commitment to their own ongoing learning. However, credibility alone does not suffice. Authenticity, a word much bandied about these days, resides in the rabbis' ability to manifest open-minded and nonjudgmental responses to their learners. This stance is grounded in the rabbis' capacity to continue to empathically confront, examine, and reflect upon the meaning that the texts suggest for *their* own lives, just as they encourage their learners to do likewise. Authenticity also includes the rabbis' invitation to their learners, through verbal and nonverbal cues, to raise concerns, pose questions, offer perspective, and solicit opinions. Together the rabbis and their learners generate interpretations and understanding of Jewish texts. In so doing they refresh the meaning of ancient sources.

To facilitate as a guide means that the exploration of Jewish texts happens in a way that makes expert knowledge accessible rather than esoteric. It puts the focus on the adults developing their own knowledge, comprehension, and interpretation of these texts, rather than on the rabbi's expertise. Of special importance, yet again, is trust. In this instance, trust requires that the rabbis do not use text study as part of a covert or overt attempt to coerce, pressure, or otherwise ideologically indoctrinate their learners. Even when the rabbis present a particular viewpoint, they do so in a manner that encourages the learners to make their own decisions and informed choices. This process happens by asking the learners to share and reflect upon their experiences and perspectives; doing so is integral to any exploration of a text. It also occurs by the rabbis modeling their cognitive and affective processes in response to the texts. In both instances, the rabbis demonstrate that they want the learners to arrive at their own ideas, even as they discover the rich range of interpretive and narrative voices of several millennia of a text-based religious tradition.

These issues are not exclusive to Jewish clergy as educators. Clergy who care about teaching their tradition through interpretive textual study face a demanding challenge. Rowell discussed the need for Christian clergy to help adult learners see their own experiences reflected through the process of studying sacred texts. His observations apply to Jewish clergy as well:

> If it is true that the typical congregant today is biblically illiterate and even less informed about the language of faith in the larger religious community, the minister's challenge is to teach the tradition in a way that helps persons make sense of their personal and social experience in light of the gospel. And the reverse is true. As global events unfold, the minister seeks to bring that world to the people through the eyes of critical/biblical/theological reflection to help them grapple with the questions and issues those events pose for the religious community. (2000, 75)

To a certain extent Rowell's remarks mirror Eric's definition of the correct meaning of the Hebrew term *Torah l'shmah*, which usually translates as "studying Torah for its own sake." In his remarks to me about teaching Torah, Eric expressed the view that paradoxical as it may initially appear, *Torah l'shmah* study should lead us to face the most fundamental issues about our humanity. In his words: "To get us in touch with the meaning of why we're here." As religious educators, the rabbis guide their learners through an interpretive process. It is one that invites learners to understand how such texts become sources of connection and insight. The texts exist in relation to a faith tradition, but most especially in dialogue with the learners' lived experiences.

Teaching Bible

All three rabbis teach Tanakh (Hebrew Bible). Barry Holtz's 2003 book, *Textual Knowledge: Teaching the Bible in Theory and Practice*, offers a helpful frame for understanding their approaches. Holtz's book does not address teachers of adults or rabbis, but it provides instructive insights for any educators who teach the Bible. Holtz drew on Stanford education scholar Pamela Grossman's concept of teaching orientations (1991). According to Grossman, "an orientation towards literature represents a basic organizing framework for knowledge about literature" (1991, 248). Grossman created her taxonomy for English teachers, and Holtz built on it by applying it to the Bible (see table on next page). Holtz defined an orientation as "a teacher's most powerful conceptions and beliefs about the field he or she is teaching" (2003, 48–49). While Grossman proposed three orientations (reader, text, and context) for teaching English literature, Holtz identified nine for Jewish texts. These bear a relationship to Grossman's three but find a unique home by linking biblical theory, theories of teaching, and Holtz's innovative biblical pedagogy.

None of the rabbis in this book mentioned any familiarity with Holtz's ideas. While all of them referred in passing to theories of biblical interpretation (and Rina even included one such book, Richard Elliott Friedman's *Who Wrote the Bible*, in her weekly Torah study), they made no reference to exploring theories about how to teach the Bible in any of our interviews. It is an example of how rabbis and other adult religious educators would benefit by familiarity with current educational scholarship. Such familiarity would enable them to frame their teaching of a sacred text in more than an idiosyncratic or individualized manner. It would also enable them to see patterns that transcend any particular teacher's method, ones that are grounded in deeply held philosophical and moral positions about the value

BIBLE ORIENTATION	KEY ELEMENT	EXAMPLES	WHERE FOUND?
Contextual	Bible in the context of its own times	Academic research on Bible—historically oriented studies	Universities, secular schools in Israel
Literary Criticism	Tools of modern literary criticism applied to the Bible	Academic research on the Bible—literary critical studies; sometimes in textbooks	Universities; some (usually) non-Orthodox schools
Reader-Response	Tools of post-modern literary criticism applied to the Bible	Academic research on the Bible—literary critical studies; sometimes in textbooks	Universities; some (usually) non-Orthodox schools
Parshanut, (Jewish Interpretive)	Exploration of classical commentators' understanding of Bible	Nehama Leibowitz as a model	Schools of various sorts, though mainly Orthodox; rarely in universities
Moralistic-Didactic	What is the moral lesson that the Bible teaches us?	Textbooks	Schools of various sorts, both Orthodox and non-Orthodox
Personalization	How can the Bible speak to us—psychologically, politically, spiritually?	Usually not in curriculum materials—found in contemporary works on the Bible	Schools of various sorts
Ideational	What are the "big ideas" of the Bible?	Melton curriculum as a model	Schools, mainly non-Orthodox
Bible Leads to Action	Study leads us to performing commandments; ethical behavior	Found in textbooks of various sorts	Schools of various sorts
Decoding, Translating, and Comprehension	Decoding in Hebrew, comprehending the basics	Found in older textbooks	All schools

Holtz 2003, 95. Used by permission of the publisher and the author.

of the Bible as a holy book. It would invite them to reflect upon their practice. It might motivate them to discuss with colleagues and learners the implications of different interpretive stances toward the text. Finally, it would act as an invitation for them to experiment with different approaches, thereby allowing them to stretch their teaching in new ways.

My interviews, observations, and personal correspondence indicate that the rabbis favor (unconsciously, given what was just written above) certain orientations over others. These inclinations are likely linked to their own preferences when studying and interpreting sacred texts. Crucially, they also appear to be shaped by their perceptions of how adults benefit most from text study. All three rabbis showed evidence of employing the Reader-Response orientation. Otherwise, they varied in the preferred orientations. Rina showed a marked preference for the Reader-Response orientation and the Personalization orientations. These orientations correspond to her emphasis on connections. Jonathan emphasized the Reader-Response orientation, the Personalization orientation, the Ideational orientation, and the Bible Leads to Action orientation. These orientations reflect his focus on personal relevance. Eric relied upon the Contextual orientation, the Literary Criticism orientation, the Reader-Response orientation, and the Ideational orientation. These orientations correspond to his interest in the deeper historical and philosophical meaning (in his words, "generating understanding") that can be achieved through learning.

Evaluating their teaching of the Bible in light of Holtz's theory suggests that an ability to modify their repertoire of orientations could enhance their learners' experiences. For example, in Rina and Jonathan's classes, learners in their sixties and older sometimes asked questions about the historical background and historical verifiability of the Bible. Both rabbis were clear in the interviews and observations that they did not want to spend a great deal of time on these historical issues. They believed that they reflected a literalist reaction that was often grounded in childhood education. However, they also understood that for many adults the historical validity of the text was a perplexing dilemma. This confusion was true especially in relation to faith in God and religious belief. An awareness of Holtz's orientations might enable them to be more ready to honor that dilemma, address it, and show how it ties in to other ways of approaching the Bible. These could include options that are, in their view, more developmentally suited to adult religious learning.

In Eric's case, his natural inclination toward analytical thinking and his scholarly background sometimes obscured his expressed goal of generating understanding. For example, in his Bible class on King David's final days from the First Book of Samuel, Eric mentioned aging and generational relationships in passing. The majority of learners in that group were older retirees. Using the Personalization orientation may have helped draw them into the text more fully.

In sum, would knowledge about the range of orientations help the rabbis become more responsive to their learners' interest in the Bible—even when it may not be the main focus of study? Would an ability to offer different paradigms of interpretation through the orientations demonstrate the kind of respect for their learners that the rabbis so value and honor in their teaching? Would it open new ways for their learners to understand the complexity of the Bible as a piece of great literature, no less than as a sacred book? My answer to all these questions, framed by the rabbi's desire to be facilitators is: Yes, it probably would. Knowledge of the range of Holtz's orientations would, at the very least, provide them with a chance to reflect on their educational philosophies when teaching the Bible. It would, in all likelihood, give them a broader theoretical framework for approaching any particular topic within the Bible. While already highly successful in linking sacred text study to existential and transcendent concerns, an awareness of current educational theories such as Holtz's would surely improve their knowledge in the area of facilitating text study.

FACILITATOR SUMMARY

The facilitator role exemplifies the range and depth of Jonathan, Rina, and Eric's teaching practice. Being approachable, moderating discussion, modeling open-ended questioning, and guiding text study incorporate a variety of strategies that support an egalitarian teaching ethos rather than a hierarchical one. At the center of this repertoire, however, reside several deeply embedded values. These include an embrace of a democratic learning environment, an appreciation of the complexity of Jewish tradition, and a commitment to the dignity of every learner. Trust is at the heart of this value system.

In Judaism, one of the Hebrew words for faith in God is *emunah*; although sometimes translated into English as "belief," a better translation is trust. According to the *Encyclopaedia Judaica*, "the verb *he'emin* . . . the noun *'emunah* ... mean to trust and have confidence; and faithfulness; and in this sense are used both of God and of man (Gen 15:6; Deut 32:4; Prov 20:6; Job 4:18)" (2007, 290). The quality of trust that the rabbis cultivate in their teaching reflects a profoundly spiritual orientation toward their interactions with their learners. Through such *emunah,* they bring a sacred dimension to their role as facilitators. It is one, moreover, whose sources reach deep into the heart of Judaism's awareness of the holiness in our relations with God and with our fellow human beings.

The Constellation

Emunah allows the rabbis to take their learners on a journey. Study of Judaism's sacred narratives opens a way to new exploration and interpretation when adults encounter them with a spirit of honest inquiry. *Emunah* gives the learners safety in their relationship with their rabbi and fellow learners. This safety encourages the learners to reveal their hearts and minds. It also gives them the chance to contemplate transformations in their perspectives about Judaism without judgment or coercion from a religious authority figure. It cultivates the awareness that the journeys we embark upon for answers to our most profound concerns as human beings can be enriching spiritual adventures. This experience can imbue our daily existence with strength and hope even as we wrestle with our all too human insecurities and doubts. As facilitators, the rabbis help the learners trust in the journeys that they undertake together through learning.

FACILITATOR CHECKLIST

- How do I create trust with my adult learners?
- Am I approachable in my interactions with adults? What specific examples can I find of that approachability in past dealings?
- What decisions do I make before teaching that help promote discussion among the learners?
- How do I actively demonstrate respect for learners whose ideas differ from mine?
- How do I share my textual expertise and respect my learners' voices?

chapter 6

RABBIS AS CO-LEARNERS

In Jewish tradition, learning is not only a valorized lifelong behavior, but also, if not more so, a religious commandment. The daily liturgy includes passages from the Talmud affirming that Torah study is equivalent to many of the most essential ethical commandments because of its beneficial effect on morality (*b. B. Shabbat* 127a). Learning, according to the Talmud, spurs redemptive action (*b. B. Kid.* 40b). Of various metaphorical crowns described in the Talmud (Priesthood, Kingship, and Torah), the crown of Torah, or study, is available to all people (*b. B. Yoma* 72b). While the Talmud insists that daily time needs to be scheduled for study, the sages acknowledge the temptation to delay. Chapter 2 of *Ethics of the Fathers* records their colleague Hillel reminding his followers: "Do not say when I have leisure I will study; perchance you may never have leisure" (*m.* 5). In the Talmud even God spends time studying (*b. B. Av. Zar.* 3b).

When rabbis say that they are teachers, it is easy to forget that embedded in that identity is a commitment to learning as a sacred activity. The expertise that comes from many years of seminary education is only the beginning of a rabbinic identity as an educator, one that ideally is infused with an ongoing passion for learning. Yet, even so, the honorific of Rabbi may convey the impression to the laity that most of a rabbi's learning has been achieved as a seminary student. For rabbis, the leadership, administrative, and pastoral demands of the rabbinate may leave them too little time to study regularly.

Jonathan, Rina, and Eric emphasize the importance of a commitment to ongoing learning to their rabbinate. Their teaching styles reflect the idea of "personal modeling" (Grasha 1996, 154).[1] They model learning as a collaborative, sacred process. As co-learners they powerfully articulate their religious and spiritual journeys even as they authoritatively guide their adult learners.

For all three, the themes of exploration and discovery as a religious pursuit propel their teaching. In his essay "Empowering Images of the Minister as Teacher," J. C. Rowell employed the image of a co-learner as one of seven metaphors to describe the minister as a teacher. He explained: "The sharp teacher/student dichotomy is a false one, especially in the church, in which the teacher is the minister and the laity are the students. For what is to be taught and learned is a way of life that is shared between minister and people" (2000, 73). Jonathan, Rina, and Eric each referred to the high priority they place on their identity as co-learners for similar reasons to those Rowell identified.

In the context of higher education, Belenky and her colleagues in *Women's Way of Knowing* referred to the related idea of "connected teaching" (1986). Like Rowell's description, connected teaching transforms the hierarchical division between teacher and learner into a more symmetrical partnership among adults. As a foundational text for studying gender in higher education, *Women's Way of Knowing* rejected the expert-novice hierarchy that conventionally fits descriptions of traditionally male-dominated higher education. Instead, the authors proposed that adult women in particular, but not exclusively, will let go of what they described as "learned silence" and claim their voices only through a shift in a hierarchical relationship. Instead of power informed by superior knowledge as the determining factor, they argued for a foundation built upon reciprocal respect between teacher and adult learners.

Although none of the rabbis in this book mentioned the work of Belenky and her colleagues, their understanding of the relational dynamics in an educational setting reflects the spirit of reciprocity evoked by *Women's Way of Knowing*. Furthermore, in their embrace of a teaching style that presents learning as a communal sacred activity, the rabbis display coherence between their teaching aspirations and their practice. A clearly articulated vision that places learning at the center of Jewish living is a key to their

---

1. The following definition of teaching style will be used in this chapter: "Teaching style is the study of matching teaching beliefs and values—the philosophy of the individual—with the behaviors used in the teaching-learning exchange" (Heimlich and Norland 2002, 19, 23).

success as rabbinic teachers. The congruence between vision and practice resembles Chris Argyris and Donald Schoen's analysis of "espoused theory" and "theory-in-use" in professional practice (1974). Argyris argued that the greater the congruence between espoused theories—what people believe they do in their work— and theories in use—what people actually do in their work— the more effective the practice (1980). For Jonathan, Rina, and Eric, several core orientations in their teaching styles as co-learners underlie their approach. They are addressed in the remainder of this chapter.

SHARING PERPLEXITIES

Eric invoked the phrase "sharing perplexities" in our interviews, but it applies to all three rabbis inasmuch as they value including their own exploration about the complexities in Judaism, Jewish tradition, and Jewish texts when they teach. Their education and erudition do not endow them with absolute and final certainty. On the contrary, they gravitate toward the reality that to live as a committed, knowledgeable Jew entails confronting and struggling with theology, religion, spirituality, ethics, history, and ritual. Taking Judaism seriously means being willing to navigate paradox and tension. Exploring the dilemmas and contradictions in Jewish texts, Jewish belief, and Jewish practice becomes part of leading a purposeful Jewish life. Each of the three rabbis discussed the challenging encounters between Judaism and contemporary realities. How do adults traverse the distance that often exists between the imperatives of an ancient tradition and the new insights of the present day? This question confronts them regularly. Three noteworthy examples illustrate how the rabbis address these matters as educators.

Sexual Orientation

In our first interview Eric described how as a congregational rabbi, he faced the issue of homosexuality. Jewish law, Jewish practice, Jewish identity, new understandings of homosexuality, and communal inclusion and exclusion all drew his attention to this subject. Despite initial resistance, he began a step-by-step process with the congregation to learn about the implications of changing communal attitudes toward homosexuality. He brought his questions and his evolving perspective to the congregation for dialogue with the membership. Rabbis in Conservative synagogues have final say on a wide range of matters. Eric decided, however, that it was preferable to study with his congregation. This was not the first time that he had chosen such a path (see chapter 4). To include laity in an ongoing exploration of a controversial subject about which he had not yet reached any final conclusions infused a participatory dynamic into what easily could have become a hierarchical one.

Gender and Misogyny

Early in her rabbinate Rina underwent a period of disruptive doubting about classical rabbinic Judaism's attitudes toward women. She described the potential personal and professional crisis it precipitated and how it was resolved (see chapter 3). In subsequent observations I witnessed her discussions with learners about gendered images of God in Jewish literature. She took up the subject of misogynist attitudes toward women in Jewish tradition. During our interviews and in her courses, I frequently heard her reiterate to her learners her belief that no religious system has a monopoly on truth. She invites the learners to consider the implications of this outlook with regard to Judaism, gender, and their own Jewish attachments.

Jewish Ethics

In a number of my observations I saw that Jonathan repeatedly discussed the unethical behavior narrated in the biblical stories about patriarchs, matriarchs, and their families. He connected the theme of unethical behavior to issues in contemporary society. He admitted to his learners that it was a subject that caused him distress. He wondered how they dealt with public reports of Jews behaving immorally. Did they feel shame as members of a minority ethnic and religious group? Did they talk about it with their Jewish and non-Jewish acquaintances? Should one person be held up as an example of an entire group? He delved into biblical sources with his learners to discover timeless truths about human imperfection, God's judgment and forgiveness, and Judaism's ethical imperatives.

Judaism Is Complex and Evolving

When rabbis openly "share their perplexities" as co-learners, they function on several planes. They reveal their personal experiences, their emotional responses, and their intellectual wrestling. They demonstrate how they have initiated their own process of reflection. They encourage learners to do so as well. Rabbis also recognize the risks involved in such an undertaking. High among them may be unsettling their learners' entrenched beliefs about Judaism. However, they find it necessary. This undertaking must be pursued in a setting in which trust in the rabbi's sincerity promotes commitment and honesty. The challenge then enriches the learners rather than precipitating feelings of alienation or threat.

The process bridges experiential, religious, spiritual, and intellectual domains. In their interviews the rabbis frequently cited stories of their interactions with adult learners about difficult topics. These anecdotes displayed an awareness of the influence that such modeling can have on their adult learners' ability to imagine Judaism as a complex and evolving religious tradition. It becomes a faith toward which they can bring the fullness of their adult selves. These selves wrestle with the complexity of modernity in core domains of the lives, from family relationships, to politics, to finances, as constructive-developmental psychologist Robert Kegan has pointed out in his influential scholarship (1986; 1994; see chapter 1). If Judaism is to become central rather than peripheral, adult learners benefit by learning how to wrestle with it. As co-learners, the rabbis provide them with a teacher who will model possible ways to do so, rather than providing them with preordained solutions.

EMBRACING DIFFICULT QUESTIONS

Sharing perplexities frequently leads the rabbis to present the adult learners with difficult questions about Jewish tradition. In turn, study with their rabbis prompts the learners to ask these kinds of questions. Such questions defy easy, immediate, clear, or final answers. Difficult questions include two different categories that sometimes overlap. One category includes questions that emerge during text study. The other encompasses questions that come from the rabbis' and learners' experiences or current concerns. They cover intellectual, ethical, spiritual, religious, theological, and historical issues.

Controversial topics that emerge during Torah study, such as biblical attitudes toward women, God-commanded violence, ethnocentrism, homophobia, and the theological implications of the Holocaust are examples of such topics. Comparative religion and the historical evolution of theology in Judaism are other areas that trigger discussions about difficult questions. During my observations these issues served as springboards for asking difficult questions. I witnessed Rina and Jonathan field frequent inquiries about the truth of the historical narrative in the Bible. In classes that addressed God's actions in history—in particular those that led to discussions about the religious and theological implications of the Holocaust—the rabbis did not shy away from engaging the learners. Furthermore, they encouraged such questions.

By posing difficult questions, the rabbis aspire to present Judaism as a rich and multivocal religion. They reject the portrayal of Judaism as a static, unchanging system. The rabbis view Jewish tradition as complex and evolving. They search out the diverse meanings embedded in and emerging from ancient texts. They willingly confront problematic ethical, philosophical, theological, historical, and personal subjects. As co-learners, the rabbis welcome the questions that their learners pose as part of a larger matrix of religious, spiritual, and existential seeking. Certainly they are more knowledgeable than their learners about Judaism. But their knowledge gives them the expertise to expose the difficulties, even as they bring their own processes of reflection to the learning environment.

Reflection becomes essential to this kind of collaborative learning. It includes the rabbis' ability to model for their learners that anyone who engages in learning has a right and even an obligation to make decisions about possible answers to the questions that are asked. The answers are sometimes tentative. They may change over time, but to pose difficult questions reflects honesty, integrity, and respect for oneself, one's community, and the tradition to which one belongs. Such an approach to teaching underscores the crucial place that critical reflection occupies in the rabbis' teaching style (Brookfield 1986; Mezirow 1990). According to Mezirow, critical reflection is a process of "reflection on presuppositions" (Mezirow 1990, 6). These presuppositions determine a person's beliefs and behaviors. Critical reflection is vital to transformational learning: "Uncritically assimilated meaning perspectives, which determine what, how, and why we learn, may be transformed through critical reflection" (1990, 18). Brookfield similarly defined critical reflection as a process through which adults learn to analyze the contextual basis of their experiences and ideas. This process is a precondition for personal and societal change (2000, 126). Cranton, another prominent theorist of transformational learning theory, described critical reflection as the "central process in transformative learning" (1996, 79).

Critical reflection is fundamental to Jonathan, Rina, and Eric's teaching styles as co-learners. They employ it to confront problematic aspects of Judaism and Jewish history. These are areas that provoke for the learners and the rabbis "disorienting dilemmas" or "problems" within Jewish life, to borrow terminology from Cranton and Mezirow (Mezirow 1990; Cranton 1996). Such modeling opens new perspectives for the learners. It demonstrates a bold and frank way of encountering the many paradoxes that moderns face as they discover an ancient tradition in conversation with contemporary realities. An open inquiry style encourages learners to investigate their beliefs and biases (their own and those embedded in Jewish texts and tradition). At the same time, it affirms the ability to remain deeply connected to tradition precisely through such confrontation.

This kind of a teaching style, however, has the potential to create conflict. Rabbis need to attend to those learners for whom the process becomes potentially too disruptive. What happens when it risks threatening rather than strengthening their adult learners' sense of Jewish connection? It is for this reason, among others (discussed in the previous chapter and in the next one), that ongoing learning in a community is essential. Learning like this best succeeds in an environment in which a relationship with the teacher and with other learners extends beyond a class session. The rabbis' regular presence in their lives helps the learners move through any conflicts that may be provoked. One-on-one follow-up opportunities matter as a result. It is why communal gatherings in which congregants socialize informally and when subjects can be pursued at further length on an as-desired basis are vital to the learning, rather than pleasant but superfluous.

Still, there are instances when the approach becomes too disturbing for some learners. For example, Eric told me about a congregant who had been learning with him, but who began to object to Eric's teaching. He wanted answers more than questions. He was disgruntled with Eric as a result. Although Eric sympathized with the congregant, in private conversations with him he was frank about his understanding of Judaism and the goals of Jewish learning. The learner eventually left the congregation for a community that gave him what he needed as a learner.

Another challenge to asking difficult questions comes from adult learners who prefer their rabbinic teachers to be expert lecturers. A frontal rabbinic teaching style traces its origins to two sources: the congregational rabbi's authority as sermon-deliverer and the rabbi-as-scholar's position as subject-area expert. Such a presence certainly has its place in adult education and in adult Jewish learning (Farrah 1991; Flexner 1995). However, Jonathan, Rina, and Eric do not view it as fundamental to their teaching. In many ways, it even undermines their purposes. Lecturing defeats the underlying premise of rabbis as co-learners. Rather, to be a co-learner evokes one signature mode of traditional Jewish education: studying sacred texts in a group, and especially in pairs with a peer in the study house, also known in Hebrew as *Havruta* (Holzer and Kent 2014).

Jewish culture traditionally extols learning as a communal activity. For example, the Talmud affirms that it is by virtue of group learning that one properly understands Torah. The word used to describe this group study is *haburah* (b. B. Ber. 63b). The root of *Haburah* is identical with that of *havruta—haver*. In English this word translates loosely into "friend." While historians debate the origins of *havruta* as a pedagogical orientation, since the start of the twentieth century it traces its beginnings to the traditional study centers of Torah learning in Eastern Europe (Schultz). It stands in vivid contrast to more conventional understandings of the rabbi's historical role in American synagogues. When Jonathan, Rina, and Eric perceive themselves as co-learners, they invoke within the contemporary liberal synagogue a practice that links them and their learners to Jews who in earlier eras and even today live and learn very differently. To the extent that they view asking difficult questions as integral to their teaching style, they evoke age-old talmudic methods of questioning. As such, it would not be an exaggeration to say that as co-learners they embody the paradox of being radical and traditional simultaneously.

LISTENING

Fundamental to being co-learners who share perplexities and pose difficult questions is modeling how to listen. The skills required for listening cannot be overstated. Nor can the outcomes for their learners. As listeners, the rabbis participate in discussions rather than dominate them. They show their willingness to learn from fellow adults. These adults include those who possess even minimal formal Jewish textual knowledge, but whose secular learning, life experiences, and personal motivation enrich the study. Moreover, the rabbis create a forum for the learners' personal narratives to be voiced. Listening encourages the learners to actively engage with each other as much as they do with the rabbi. The knowledge gained is part of a dynamic whereby the rabbis seek to generate critical reflection, personal relevance, and communal participation. Transmission of a predetermined content over a specified period of time through lecture or a drive to cover a preset curriculum is not the dominant concern of the rabbis. Most of the adult study groups do not have a fixed start or end date.

The ability to listen illuminates the concept of "real talk" developed by Belenky and her colleagues (1986, 144–46). They described it "as a way of connecting to others and acquiring and communicating new knowledge ... they [the teachers] question and listen to others, urging them to speak, so that they might better know the world from the other person's vantage point" (ibid., 145). In Schuster and Grant's application of Jane Vella's theories to adult Jewish learning, the authors identified several central components of creating "sound relationships" between the teacher and the learner. Prominent among them was the ability to generate a feeling of "teamwork" in the adult Jewish learning setting. Doing so calls for the educator to listen (2005, 144).

Jonathan, Rina, and Eric listen to the responses to the topic being discussed with an awareness of and sensitivity to the learner's Jewish background and life experiences. They listen to the direction of the unfolding discussion within the group. They mirror back to the learners what they hear. They reflect on it afterward independently or with colleagues. They follow up on this reflection by introducing any appropriate or relevant issues into subsequent teaching-learning encounters.

Interpersonal concerns, such as whether one of the learners may be dominating the discussion, also require an ability to listen attentively. When to decide how far the discussion may go beyond what the rabbis find helpful to the learning is another area of focused listening. Choosing to continue or redirect the discussion involves the capacity to listen in the ways described above. Listening also reveals the value placed on the learners' interactions with each other, rather than directing their comments primarily toward the rabbi.

The practice of this kind of listening may run counter to many stereotypical views of clergy identity. Understandings of rabbis as preachers, life-cycle officiants, pastoral counselors, and teachers generate the idea of a religious authority figure who remains apart from the laity. The expert transmits wisdom and guidance verbally through speech. Where does listening enter? Jonathan, Rina, and Eric counter this perception. Through their ability to listen, they model a different kind of rabbinic presence.

When rabbis listen they bring a powerful aspect of Judaism to their teaching. Classical rabbinic tradition requires Jews to recite the prayer known as the *Sh'ma* three times a day. Of biblical origin, the *Sh'ma*, as a declaration of God's oneness, is expressed as an instruction to listen through the Hebrew word *sh'ma* whose root translates as "listen." To experience the unity that spirits creation as expressed through one God, tradition commands that Jews listen. Addressed initially in Deuteronomy (6:4–9) to the community at large, it suggests that listening is also a fundamental communal spiritual practice.

In a subsequent biblical passage in Kings I, we find the famous story of the prophet Elijah's encounter with God. The Rosh Hashanah and Yom Kippur liturgies incorporate this section into their penitential prayers. The verse *"kol de'mama daka"*—translated as a still small voice—describes how Elijah heard God's voice (19:12). Hearing God's voice requires careful listening. It is no coincidence that the narrative excerpt appears during a season deeply invested with spiritual introspection and communal penitence. At this time of year tradition obligates Jews to listen to the blowing of the *shofar*, or ram's horn. Symbolic interpretations of the religious ritual include how doing so is intended to awaken us to our flaws no less than to our aspirations for repentance and renewal.

Theologically, these biblical sources and the liturgical rituals that accompany them highlight the spiritual power inherent in listening. Listening expresses more than sound educational practice. It contains within it the energy of Jewish tradition. It expresses a deep strand in Judaism that seeks God's presence through listening. When Jonathan, Rina, and Eric listen as co-learners, they frame their work as rabbis within the context of Judaism's call to hear God's voice abiding among us and within us.

SUPPORTING ADULT DEVELOPMENT

When Jonathan, Rina, and Eric listen, they show their intuitive sensitivity to the influence of adult development on their teaching. Developmental awareness spans psychological, sociocultural, and cognitive domains. Adult development affects learning. Likewise, learning often influences development. Research in adult education and adult Jewish learning repeatedly addresses the relationship between adult development and adult learning (see chapter 1).

Jewish adults sometimes turn to learning because of a substantive change in their lives, such as a move, a loss of a job, a divorce, or the death of a loved one. This upheaval prompts them to seek new connections or contact with Judaism (Schuster 2005). Kegan's constructive-developmental theory in relation to adult development provides insight into the rabbis' perception of their role as co-learner amidst the demands of adulthood (1994; 2000). In describing the stressors of modernity and postmodernity, Kegan wrote:

> Unlike traditionalism, in which a fairly homogeneous set of definitions of how one should live is consistently promulgated by the cohesive arrangements, models, and codes of the community or tribe, modernism is characterized by ever-proliferating pluralism, multiplicity, and competition for our loyalty to a given way of living. Modernism requires that we be more than well socialized; we must also develop the internal authority to look at and make judgments about the expectations and claims that bombard us from all directions. Yet adult learners today and tomorrow encounter not only the challenges of modernism but of postmodernism as well. Postmodernism calls on us to win some distance even from our own internal authorities so that we are not completely captive of our own theories, so that we can recognize their incompleteness, so that we can even embrace contradictory systems simultaneously. (2000, 68)

As adults, the three rabbis also experience the complexities that Kegan described, just as their learners do. Rina and Eric were in their late fifties at the time of the research. Jonathan had just turned forty. Perceiving themselves as co-learners reflects an implicit awareness on their part that like their adult learners, they, too, are moving through the developmental processes and demands associated with different phases of adulthood. Conceptualizing the rabbi's role as a co-learner in light of adult developmental theory is an area ripe for further research in the domain of rabbinic identity more generally.

The rabbis' capacity for reflection about their own educational and Jewish journeys was revealing in this regard. In our interviews they described times in their adult lives when they faced conflicts and decisions that affected their perspectives, beliefs, and choices in relation to Judaism. These experiences in turn helped them empathize with the developmental concerns articulated by their learners. A few examples related to transitional periods for the rabbis are illustrative in this regard.

Life Transitions

Jonathan discussed the intellectual dissonance he experienced when he learned about the discrepancy between traditional religious explanations of biblical historicity and academic scholarship about the Bible during rabbinical school. The challenges to his religious beliefs forced him to step back from assumptions that he had held to be true for his entire life until that time. He also spoke about how he and his wife dealt with creating a Jewish home as Reform Jews. He described the maturation process that it entailed for them as a couple. They worked deliberately to find the balance between their passionate commitment to Jewish ritual, a flexible approach to practice, and participation in an open American society.

Eric talked about the transformation he underwent in his forties. His awareness of having reached a midway point in his life and the accompanying existential concerns it raised motivated him to leave academia. A primary outcome included applying for the position at Beth Shalom. In addition, as a congregational rabbi, he emphasized his growing awareness that he personally needed a more spiritually centered Judaism. He undertook outside learning with a cohort of rabbis through a Jewish organization. He began to experiment with means to bring his search to his congregants. He invited those who felt similarly to participate in new prayer and learning initiatives.

The rabbis' willingness to reflect upon these experiences and life passages and to consider how they influenced them as rabbis brings the importance of their own developmental trajectory into focus. In the interviews the rabbis displayed an intuitive sensitivity as adult educators to the importance of adult development. These insights suggest an implicit grasp of the cognitive and psychosocial challenges faced by rabbis and their learners. That the rabbis have an opportunity to get to know their learners in settings beyond the learning groups, such as in pastoral counseling and life-cycle events, also sensitized them to their learners' developmental trajectories.

Know and Respect Your Congregants

Jonathan remarked that most of the adults in his congregation had rudimentary formal Jewish education. They felt vulnerable until they got into the habit of learning. To visibly demonstrate honor and respect for their level of learning and their ideas was important to his self-understanding as a rabbi. Rina's family-education programs include adult learning sessions before the intergenerational sessions. The themes that drive these encounters almost always integrate developmental issues in the domain of parent-child relationships with learning about Jewish texts and rituals. Her courses for women reflect the awareness that women and men sometimes have different developmental concerns. Even in an egalitarian congregation she acknowledges that some subjects are more suitable for women or men to address separately. This kind of focus grew out of her own experiences as a woman, wife, mother, and rabbi. It also was a response to the expressed needs of her female congregants.

At the same time, the three rabbis never *explicitly* identified adult development as a subject they had studied, nor did any of them mention it as a knowledge base critical to rabbis. This lacuna confirms research by Schuster on the lag time with regard to developmental understanding in adult Jewish education overall (2003). For example, although rigidly segregated birth cohorts were not evident in the rabbis' classes, in some of them a majority of the learners were in their sixties and older. This was particularly the case in the weekday morning classes offered by Eric and Jonathan. Rina also expressed some concern that over the years, people in their fifties and beyond predominated in the Shabbat morning Torah study. At the time of our interviews she was trying to design ways to attract younger adults as well.

The rabbis did not, however, approach learning in these settings much differently from those with younger adults or with a mixed group. One member of the adult education committee at Jonathan's synagogue mentioned that the younger adults who ranged from their thirties to their fifties seemed more interested than their older counterparts in learning that incorporated family issues into the themes and topics. She observed that older adults were more interested in philosophical, historical, and theological subjects. In our interviews, however, Jonathan did not point out this distinction.

Adult development research has been fundamental to adult education since it emerged as a field of scholarship and practice. From its earliest days, adult learning theory has been closely intertwined with developmental psychology. In the past few decades, new areas of research on adult education and narrative have invigorated debates about the intersection of adult learning and adult development. Faith development has attracted its share of attention by scholars and practitioners in religious education. Even those scholars who express caution or criticism about what they perceive as an overemphasis on the subject acknowledge its influence.

It is troubling that even though adult development sensitivities emerged as a central axis in the rabbis' teaching style as co-learner, none of them indicated studying adult development in seminary, nor did they refer to doing so in any subsequent capacity. Their insights accrued almost exclusively from the wisdom of practice and trial and error. While these ways of learning are valuable, they are insufficient. Given the centrality of the subject to adult education, it would seem reasonable for rabbinical students and rabbis to be exposed more fully to the richness of the literature in this area. The contrast between the importance of adult development to their practice and their lack of informed knowledge about the subject stood out as an area ripe for further investigation. The situation applies particularly in regard to seminary preparation and clergy professional development.

CO-LEARNER SUMMARY

By viewing themselves as co-learners, Jonathan, Rina, and Eric model a rabbinic identity that emphasizes humility as a moral and spiritual quality. Being a rabbi whose teaching style embodies the qualities of a co-learner requires humility. The corpus of biblical and especially rabbinic literature highly valorizes this quality as a spiritual attribute. In the biblical book of Numbers we read that Moses, described as the greatest teacher ever in Israel, was defined most prominently by his humility (12:3). According to the Talmud, of the ten degrees of moral perfection, humility ranks highest (*b. B. Av. Zar.* 20b; *Ar.* 16b). It reflects great reverence (*b. B. San.* 43b). It is the signature characteristic of the "disciples of Abraham" (*Ethics of the Fathers* ch. 5, *m.* 23.). Prophets, in order to attain inspiration, must possess humility (*b. B. Ned.* 38a). Humility helps establish an inclusive and egalitarian learning environment.

The Constellation

As members of the clergy, such humility is essential to their educator identity. Rather than reinforce a hierarchical relationship that creates dependency for their adult learners, these rabbis identify themselves as fellow Jews engaged in a transformative quest. When rabbis tell stories of their own struggles with hard issues, they open the conversation to their learners as well. When they listen attentively to the narratives of the adults, the rabbis create space for reflection on past experience in light of new knowledge.

Fresh awareness and evolving commitment grow out of this communal endeavor for both the rabbis and the learners. In the process, they pursue an ongoing discovery of self and others in relation to faith, belief, and religion. Their orientation to Judaism turns a religious system into more than a set of ethical imperatives and ritual regulations. Instead, it focuses on understanding religion as a spiritually inspired way of life. Spirit expresses itself in the continuous search for balance in the relationship between one's inner and outer worlds. It takes shape in the learners through watching how the rabbis commit themselves again and again to such a path, as well as by deciding to accompany their teachers as partners on it.

CO-LEARNER CHECKLIST

- To what extent am I willing to explore my own perplexities about our religious tradition with adult learners?
- How comfortable am I asking my adult learners and myself difficult questions?
- When I am teaching, how do I practice listening?
- What kinds of adult developmental issues or crises have I faced, and how have I dealt with them?
- How does my adult development affect my clergy identity?

chapter 7

RABBIS AS COMMUNITY BUILDERS

Listen carefully and you will hear just how frequently Americans speak about community. Its ubiquitous use in popular culture, however, suggests that it may be for many of us a cliché, devoid of anything but vague notions about group participation. At the other end of the spectrum, anthropologists, sociologists, and psychologists have studied community as a concept extensively for more than a century. The widespread attention by scholars to community has generated reams of theories.

In Judaism, three Hebrew words translate as community, each possessing slight differences in their orientation: *edah, kehillah,* and *kahal.* Sacred community, or *kehillah kedoshah,* traditionally binds Jews to a set of values and a way of life imbued with holiness. The synagogue, in Hebrew called *beit knesset,* which in English literally translates as "gathering house," is a communal institution that developed as early as the late Second Temple era in Jewish history. With the destruction of the Temple in seventy CE, it eventually became one of the focal points of Jewish communal existence throughout the world. Since the middle of the nineteenth century, it has been the centerpiece of organized Jewish life in the United States. As a gathering place for praying, learning, and socializing, synagogues reflect the highly decentralized nature of American Judaism. They also continue to bear the primary responsibility for sustaining Jewish communal life. This sociological reality is one of the reasons why surveys indicating a decline in synagogue membership inevitably set off alarm bells for those Jews concerned about the ongoing flourishing of American Judaism.

Jonathan, Rina, and Eric describe themselves as community builders, and they see their synagogues as primary addresses for that ongoing project. Their self-understanding is grounded in a long-term vision of creating flourishing Jewish communal centers. Yet they each convey a nuanced focus of emphasis when discussing community. These nuances are worth addressing because they indicate the rich variety of understandings that color each synagogue's distinctive communal culture. Crucially, community learning stimulates, shapes, and supports their respective visions.

For Jonathan, the synagogue community is a unique place and a safe haven. In his words, it must be a "warm and welcoming" refuge. A synagogue is a center where members discover and experience links between their overall lives and Judaism as a culture and a religious civilization. Learning in community gives access to this unfolding process. Learning generates new understandings of self both in the world and in relation to a faith, heritage, and tradition. These, in turn, continually revitalize synagogue community in a constructive feedback loop.

For Eric, community serves to create ideological coherence and shared understandings about a congregation's values and ideals. In a world of dizzying choices and few foundational loyalties, learning helps guide adults in making decisions about how to live. Rather than passively allowing life to unfold, learning spurs congregants to imagine and articulate a vision of who the congregation as a collective aspires to be.

For Rina, community entails creating bonds through learning. These include connections to fellow congregants and to Jewish patterns of living. Synagogue community depends and thrives upon relationships: relationships to Jewish ritual, to Jewish wisdom, to the Jewish calendar, and to each other as human beings who seek coherence and purpose in their lives.

The motor at the core of these three conceptions is education. The rabbis see the ongoing construction of community through teaching and learning as a central aim of their rabbinic mission. They lead synagogues where education and community exist in a mutually reciprocal relation to each other. To keep this motor running, they teach frequently to small- and medium-sized groups of adults. These learning groups foster personal and communal attachments. The rabbis forge strong interpersonal bonds with their learners. They create an environment that encourages relationships among the learners. These groups function as miniature communities within the larger congregation. In them the rabbis model ways of engaging with Judaism that invite and cultivate communal belonging. Because they meet regularly, the groups develop their own history. By incorporating stories (their own, their learners', and those that are part of Jewish tradition,

Jewish texts, and Jewish contemporary life), the rabbis and learners jointly craft a coherent and compelling narrative of Jewish communal life. This narrative extends beyond each group. It nourishes the synagogue's story more broadly. Learning together also empowers the adults to grow as Jews. It stimulates congregants to participate as members of a community for whom learning together infuses a sense of transcendent meaning into their lives.

LEARNING IN COMMUNITY

All three rabbis teach groups of varying size and age. In some cases, they have been meeting for a decade or more. These groups function as the focal point of the rabbis' regular teaching, even when other shorter courses are offered. The rabbis' continuous involvement promotes commitment not only to learning, but also to the people who attend. Rina expressed this sentiment most eloquently when she referred to her Shabbat morning group. She mentioned that members' absences are always noted and explained that a guiding principle is: "It's not about counting the house, it's about everyone counting." That concept applies equally to the groups led by Eric and Jonathan.

None of the rabbis expressed an overriding concern about numbers. In a typical week the attendance for Jonathan ranged from approximately thirty to sixty people; for Eric, from fifty to one hundred attendees; for Rina, from forty to seventy learners. Rather, it was getting to know the learners that mattered. Generating a feeling of camaraderie within the group as a whole also was a priority. These are congregants with whom the rabbis share experiences and ideas week in and week out in a way that they do not with other congregants. The benefits of such close and ongoing teacher-learner interactions may heighten the *rabbis'* own sense of integration into their synagogue communities. The opportunity to know and appreciate the learners as individuals and to create cohesion in the group was also remarked upon by many of the learners I spoke with informally. They viewed it as part of the richness of their experiences with the rabbis. They identified it as a key reason for continuing to return to study.

The regular gatherings provide an anchor in time for the learners and the rabbis. These are engaging, inviting, and informal settings. The rabbis support and promote respectful interaction. Because of this atmosphere, the participants feel comfortable sharing their concerns, questions, values, disagreements, and experiences. Along the way, the individual personalities of the rabbi and the learners emerge. The groups explore in depth the issues that continue to absorb them. Reflection grows out of the sustained learning.

During the courses that meet weekly or biweekly, recurring themes are pursued. The approach enables the participants to clarify their thoughts and feelings individually and as a collective. Even for the groups that meet less frequently, such as the adults-only section of the family education series that Rina teaches, the rabbi's teaching style encourages interpersonal connections. The socializing breaks that occur before and after the learning give participants a chance to converse informally with each other. The rabbis, who also interact with the learners and their families in other rabbinic capacities, use these pauses to check in with the adults about more personal matters, when appropriate.

An unanswered question, despite the rabbis' apparent lack of preoccupation with numbers, is whether there are other ways of extending the practice of community building through learning to more congregants. For example, all three rabbis emphasized the links between community building and teaching. However, only Rina had enlarged upon this value by working with the Jewish educational staff in an intentional way through her redefined position as the rabbi overseeing synagogue education writ large. Other regular initiatives, such as trips and retreats that emphasized bonding through informal and experiential learning, were another prong in her efforts. Neither Eric nor Jonathan appeared to have a collaborative strategy that included working with their clergy colleagues, the educational team, or lay leaders. Such coordinated interactions would create the opportunity for comprehensive adult education opportunities that could energize the community via learning even more expansively. Were they to undertake such a plan given their position as synagogue leaders, would it be possible to reach more adults over time? Would they, through their rabbinic work as community builders, be better able to mentor other Jewish educators, clergy, and laity within their congregations to see learning as the motor of communal life? The probable answer, given Rina's successes, is yes.

Cultivating Communal Lay Leadership Through Learning

Jonathan, Rina, and Eric foster community within their study groups through teaching that promotes a sense of belonging to an educational cohort within the larger culture of the congregation. The learning in these groups often leads to further involvement for laypersons in other areas of the synagogue, such as attending worship services regularly, going on synagogue-sponsored retreats, and traveling with the synagogue on trips overseas. Laypeople often teach each other in these settings. Participation in adult learning frequently leads to serving on the synagogue's board of trustees and on various committees. Jonathan pointedly described adult learning as an "incubator for upcoming leaders ... Learning leads to leadership and leadership leads to learning." Of the three rabbis, Rina appeared the most aware of the potential of these groups to serve as a focus for leadership formation within the congregation.

None of the rabbis, however, seemed conscious of the potential in designing a deliberate strategy whereby the members of these learning groups, or other newly created ones, are invited to develop their leadership skills through learning. Rather, it appears that the rabbis have yet to explore how the intersection of their rabbinic identity as institutional leaders and as educational leaders could extend to preparing laity to become leaders through learning. If, as Jonathan indicated, adult education functions organically as a leadership incubator, what kinds of learning might intentionally foster an interest in leading? How might the rabbis initiate opportunities for adults to collaboratively shape a distinctive leadership ethos within their synagogue that has learning as its foundation? These areas of teaching adults seem only incidentally related to their work. A greater awareness of the potential to expand and deepen community building through investing in lay leadership preparation would be one way to bolster a commitment to communal life through education.

COMMUNITY BUILDING AND NARRATIVE

Stories infuse Judaism. In the Bible and the Talmud no less than in Hasidic culture or modern American Jewish literature, narrative has influenced the processes involved in creating communal Jewish identity over time. American Jewish community innovator and educator Jonathan Woocher identified "story-telling" as part of "personal meaning making in a Jewish key" (1995, 27). He saw it as essential to generating attachment to Jewish community. Schuster cited the desire for coherence and purpose in a person's life as a primary reason for participation in adult Jewish learning (2003). She included sharing personal stories on the part of the teachers and the learners as fundamental to this process. Research by Lisa Grant and her colleagues on the Melton Mini-School adult Jewish education program suggested a correlation with the findings of the sociologist Robert Wuthnow about the importance of stories in support groups (Grant et al. 2004). According to Wuthnow, "[T]he act of sharing stories is key to the development of community within a group, as members offer up details of their personal histories as texts for examination and response" (cited in Grant et al. 2004, 134).

I, too, discovered that narrative was a primary locus of Jonathan, Rina, and Eric's teaching. As rabbinic teachers they tend to concentrate on three types of narrative:

1. Biblical, rabbinic, and later Jewish textual sources that are either the subject of study or related to it.
2. Personal narratives with Jewish or universal themes from the rabbis' and the learners' experiences.
3. Narratives from other cultures and traditions (religious and secular, textual and oral) that tie to the learning thematically.

Text study of narratives involves introducing adult learners to an interpretive process that is grounded in both traditionally Jewish and modern scholarly ways of studying sacred sources. While the textual narratives usually are the content of a particular class, course, or program, the personal narratives often function as discussion triggers for reflection. This latter approach helps the rabbis in their efforts to link learning and lived experience. Rossiter emphasized that using narrative content in adult education calls on teachers to be aware of the "relationship between the learners' self-narratives and their experiences of learning" (1999, 68). Both change and transformation, key concepts in adult learning, are influenced by the stories adults tell about themselves.

It is for this reason that teaching through narrative requires learning to listen attentively. As the learning moves back and forth between Jewish narrative sources and their learners' stories, the rabbis try to help the adults discover how experiences in their lives relate to Judaism as an evolving religious tradition. The dialogue (sometimes in the form of an argument) between the stories of our lives and the stories that are part of a cultural inheritance creates a canvas for the learners. On it they can experiment with the ways Judaism interacts with the spiritual, religious, and existential issues that they face as adults. This complex activity can be demanding for everyone. Ancient tales sometimes conflict with contemporary sensibilities. However, the awareness that the learners, and the events in their lives, are part of a long, complex, and rich Jewish narrative emerges as a powerful outcome of learning.

Sharing, listening, and reflecting on stories are, therefore, interlocking parts of an intertwined process. The learners discover that they, too, are participants, or, if you will, characters, in a drama that is several thousand years old. Memories of personal experiences are transformed into opportunities for understanding their links to the grand Jewish narratives, no less than to the more immediate ones in their own lives. Finding their place in these meta-narratives animates the rabbis no less than the learners. Learning functions as a forum for an evolving and conscious determination about their part in this ever-unfolding story.

For example, during one adult Bar and Bat Mitzvah class that Rina held in her home on the topic of Shabbat, she related the story of the year she lived in Jerusalem as a college student. She had attended Shabbat services regularly at a number of Orthodox synagogues. She described a dream that she had had during her time in Israel that pushed her to think more about certain problematic attitudes toward women in traditional Judaism. She told this story to highlight the complexity of her feelings toward Jewish tradition, even as she enthusiastically embraces the regular observance of many traditional Jewish rituals. During the course of this class, an older woman responded to Rina's story by volunteering memories of Friday night Shabbat dinners that she participated in as a young person. She reflected on the comfort of doing the same thing week after week. She wondered about the influence during childhood of the predictability of religious ritual in her family. The stories prompted further exchange about how religious ritual operates in family and communal life.

Eric often incorporated anecdotal stories into text study. In a Mishnah class preceding Hanukkah, for example, the group was focusing on the passage in the Talmud about Hanukkah. Eric mentioned that the historical origins of the story of the oil burning for eight days were nowhere to be found in the Jewish corpus. It only entered the tradition through a gloss in the short talmudic passages he was about to teach. A learner then mentioned a scene in a recently published book by Israeli author A. B. Yehoshua. It told the story of a group of Israelis living abroad in Africa who wanted to light the Hanukkah menorah. Unfamiliar with the blessings, they sought them out on a box of candles. This story, told within the context of Talmud study about the holiday, led to an extended discussion about the way traditions and the meanings embedded in them are created, sustained, transformed, lost, and sometimes recovered through narrative.

The three rabbis demonstrate the varied ways that the synagogue as a Jewish institution becomes a holder *and* a creator of stories. Both aspects are crucial to the generation and transmission of a collective identity. Individual narratives are linked to broader communal narratives. Congregants are encouraged to seek out a relationship between their lives and Jewish stories past and present. According to this argument, telling stories is part of the process of enabling Jews to "see that their personal stories are connected to traditional and historical Jewish narratives ('foundational stories') and to a living community that tells and enacts these stories" (Woocher 1995, 27). This position echoes arguments made by Rossiter regarding the interplay between "individual and cultural narratives." Rossiter wrote:

> Individual life narratives are situated within a myriad of overlapping familial, religious, socioeconomic and cultural contexts. The narrative of any individual life is an expression of, an embodiment of, these contexts and systems of meaning within which it lives . . . Every culture has a pool of acceptable narratives, a set of stories and story forms, through which human action and intent are interpreted, explained, and understood. Developmental processes involve the individual's recognition, selection, rejection, and/or adaptation of these available narrative forms as she or he constructs her or his own meaning. The intelligibility and followability of individual life narratives are assessed according to culturally shared understandings. (1999, 65–66)

Through their use of stories, the rabbis encourage the movement back and forth between individual and community development. As such, teaching with and through narrative becomes a potential crucible for the identity development of the rabbis' adult learners. Adult educational scholar William Randall called this process among adults "restorying" (1996). He proposed a four-step process undertaken by the adult educator. These steps incorporate the following aspects:

1. Providing a secure environment in which learners share.

2. Listening attentively.

3. Posing questions that help the learners see what kind of stories they are telling and the beliefs that undergird the stories.

4. Being a "co-author" (242) as the learners consider how to shape their self-narratives in ways that incorporate their new knowledge into their lives.

Randall's approach highlights the intrapersonal and interpersonal aspects of an adult educational process that integrates narrative and identity. It is also a way of proceeding that Jonathan, Rina, and Eric embrace even though they were not familiar with Randall's theory. Their position as congregational rabbis also gives them access to their learners' experiences in a way that other adult educators usually do not possess. In their capacity as lifecycle officiants and pastoral figures, all three have the chance to encounter their learners (and often other family members) in different situations and settings. As a consequence, they have a richer narrative background when interacting with their learners.

This privileged rabbinic knowledge about their learners' stories is part of the landscape of teaching in a synagogue. The rabbis' ability to draw out their learners' stories and to help them find ways to relate them to their individual and collective identities as Jews depends on the trust that develops between the rabbis and the learners inside and outside of any particular course. Author Larry Golemon in his essay "The Practice of Narrative Leadership in Ministry" identified seven steps whereby clergy lead their congregations through narrative practices to transformation (2010). In his discussion of the second step—"Hearing People's Stories and Linking Them to God's Story" (9)—he wrote:

> Weaving human stories with God's story is a natural, intuitive process for many pastors and congregational leaders. By becoming more intentional about this narrative work, pastors and leaders can invite people to identify with their own biblical and faith narratives and reframe aspects of their own lives—from hardship to hope—as part of God's ongoing story with God's people. Part of that reframing comes by connecting our sense of human relevance with the larger purpose or promise of God's time... How the deep work of stories affects human hearts is, in the end, up to God's spirit, but narrative leaders can juxtapose and weave stories in ways that create optimal conditions for the Spirit to be seen and heard. (13)

The "optimal conditions" Golemon mentioned depend upon the ability of the rabbis as spiritual and religious guides to engender confidence in their learners. That confidence builds when the rabbis show appreciation, respect, and interest in every learner's story. They include those stories listened to in the privacy of the rabbi's study and in the public venue of a learning group.

Historical Narratives and Religious Truths

One significant matter regarding narratives in Jewish sacred texts surfaced for all three rabbis. It concerns the task of guiding adult learners to distinguish between historical fact, or historicity, and what may best be described as "truth concerns" when studying the Bible. "Truth concerns" include philosophical, existential, spiritual, and religious issues. They transcend particular historical periods or historical verifiability. According to Jonathan, Rina, and Eric, many adult learners initially get stuck or distracted by their need to corroborate the historicity of biblical narratives. None of the rabbis believe that the historical angle is the focus that best benefits their learners when studying the Bible. Although acknowledging their interest and their frustration, the rabbis also want to broaden the way the learners understand the richness of the Bible as Torah, or sacred teaching. This point of view links to their interest in attending to adult development. It especially correlates with the theme that emerged during the course of my research about finding connections between sacred narratives and personal relevance.

Jonathan's distinction between historical events and existential truths that transcend particular historical epochs represents an attempt to move the adults away from a perspective that they often have carried with them since childhood (see chapter 2). He believes that the need to either legitimate or reject the historical accuracy of the Bible often psychologically blocks adult learners from approaching its narratives in new ways. Alternative understandings can help them make new connections to the themes in the text, ones that deepen their relationship to the Bible. Jonathan gave an example of how he responds to adults who have trouble valuing the Bible because it is full of scientific fallacies regarding the creation of the world. He tries to help them see that that the creation narratives were not intended as scientific treatises or as historical narratives in the way we moderns understand those concepts. Rather, he asks them to contemplate them as moral narratives. He invites them to consider how this shift in assumptions affects their response to the Bible.

All three rabbis know that letting go of assumptions that are rooted in early childhood exposure to Judaism, in particular to teachings about the Bible, is hard work. Replacing them with a more complex view of the sacred narrative tradition may initially disrupt their learners' beliefs. It often requires a fundamental change in outlook. Eventually, however, the rabbis find that it enriches the adults' ability to engage with the text on more nuanced levels. Facilitating this shift leads to a more sophisticated adult engagement with the Bible. As a result, the learners become adept at viewing it from the perspective of adult agency rather than childhood dependency.

Language

In a different but equally important area related to text study, the question of language surfaced implicitly and explicitly over the course of my research. Because the rabbis make such extensive use of Jewish texts whose original language is either Hebrew or Aramaic, language accessibility in English translations is a prerequisite for the adults. Much as the rabbis might hope and encourage their adult learners to study Hebrew (and even teach it in Eric's case), they accept that reading the sources in translation is essential for the majority of their congregants. Doing so provides the learners with a comfort that only conversing in one's native language can offer. It, therefore, eases the way into the heart of the learning. Jonathan mentioned this explicitly, but it was evident in Eric and Rina's approaches as well.

Giving adults possession of these sacred texts in their native language sends the message that knowledge of Hebrew is not required in order to feel educated or to sense oneself as fully part of Judaism or Jewish communal life. This recognition eliminates a barrier, such that adults no longer feel inauthentic because they lack knowledge of Hebrew. The stories of Jewish tradition that live in the sacred texts are not closed to them because they do not know the original language. Rather, by gaining a sense of ownership over the stories, they find greater attachment to them. The experience of mastery, in turn, leads them to feel grounded in Judaism in ways that they previously they may have believed were closed to them.

RABBIS, COMMUNITY BUILDING, AND LEARNER EMPOWERMENT

Teaching and learning through narrative triggers exploration of a range of existential issues. These vary from the spiritual and religious to the historical and linguistic. They encompass matters of personal and collective definition and identification. As a component of community building, teaching through narrative pushes the rabbis and their congregants to situate their lives within a broader canvas of Jewish identity development. Personality psychologist Dan P. McAdams has documented how the stories we tell and hear profoundly shape our identities:

> It is an individual's life story which has the power to tie together past, present, and future in his or her life. It is a story which is able to provide unity and purpose. It is a story which specifies a personalized "niche" in the adult world and a sense of continuity and sameness across situations and over time ... *Identity is a life story.* (1985, 18, emphasis original)

In the context of a community identity, the opportunity to hear one another's stories invites discovering the nexus between the personal and the communal. This discovery, in turn, leads to an increasing awareness of one's value to the community, also identified conceptually as empowerment.

Jonathan, Rina, and Eric often spoke in our interviews about empowering their learners. They frequently used the term more than once in an interview. Empowerment, like community, is a word that Americans like. It is, however, one that also carries many connotations. Judi Chamberlin, writing from a counseling perspective, indicated that the widespread use of the term in American society makes it "difficult to claim that 'empowerment' is a meaningful concept" (2009, para. 1). She identified fifteen qualities that could function as working definitions of the concept. Included among them were "having decision-making power, seeing things differently, effecting change in one's life and one's community." She also observed that empowerment is a relational concept, an insight that resonates with how the rabbis view empowering their adult learners through education.

To Jonathan, empowerment means connecting Judaism to personal relevance. Adults see the links between Jewish learning, personal experiences, and the choices they make about how to live their lives as Jewish human beings. In Rina's view, empowerment means that adult congregants learn how to forge connections between Jewish tradition, Jewish wisdom,

Jewish texts, Jewish rituals, and their lives. These connections nurture and sustain them and their community. For Eric, empowerment means that the collaborative investigation of Jewish texts and topics generates understanding. Understanding leads to coherence, insight, and even wisdom. In each instance, empowerment is a process of gaining increasing self-awareness that is not isolated but rather is intertwined with one's sense of connectedness to a larger whole. In this way, communal study provokes a feeling of actively belonging to one's synagogue community.

As a result, adult learning often leads to a shift in the learners' sense of their capabilities as Jews, both individually and communally. Brookfield included it as one of the six primary "principles of effective practice" of facilitation in adult learning:

> The aim of facilitation is the nurturing of self-directed, empowered adults. Such adults will see themselves as proactive, initiating individuals engaged in a continuous re-creation of their personal relationships, work worlds, and social circumstances rather than as reactive individuals, buffeted by uncontrollable forces of circumstance. (1986, 11)

The rabbis consistently refrain from conveying any kind of prescriptive messages regarding Jewish religious practices or behaviors. Yet it is possible to find in their emphasis on empowerment the hope that adult Jewish learning will lead to a heightened sense of personal religiosity and spirituality. Through the possibility of an increasing commitment to Jewish communal rhythms, the rabbis see learning as far more than an intellectual endeavor. There is an aspiration that they model about one's religious and spiritual development: participation in synagogue life is a value embedded within the learning process. Studying encourages a movement toward exploration of various aspects of the synagogue community.

Of the three rabbis, Rina illustrated this stance most clearly in her repeated return to the importance of Shabbat. Indeed, for all of the rabbis, a focus on Shabbat as a mainstay of Jewish spirituality and communal life was a topic that occupied their attention. The subject surfaced in our interviews and in their teaching. Consistent with their intuitive grasp of adult development, however, their forays were marked by gentle encouragement. They were grounded in the rabbis' willingness to speak from their own experiences. They grew out of their ability to generate trust with their congregants.

The embrace of empowerment by the rabbis speaks to the transformative aims of adult learning. Transformation happens both internally and relationally. These two dimensions are intertwined in subtle ways. To borrow language from Rina, learners come to understand themselves as givers and receivers. To choose to give one's talents, knowledge, and commitment to the community means sustaining a tradition and contributing one's own legacy to it—in other words, to be aware of one's generativity. To receive from one's rabbi and fellow congregant-learners demonstrates openness to the wisdom, insights, and care that nourish both inner life and communal relationships.

COMMUNITY BUILDER SUMMARY

Community building expresses an overarching aim of the rabbis' teaching. It is here where their identities as synagogue leaders and religious educators merge most evidently. As teachers who emphasize education as the motor of community building, Jonathan, Rina, and Eric bring a deliberatively collaborative spirit to their teaching. The work of community building reveals the democratic ethos inherent in their facilitator and co-learners roles. It orients their learners towards a sense of adult agency. As givers and receivers within their synagogues, adults discover that learning can transform them. It empowers them to contribute to the vitality of their communities.

As rabbinic teachers who seek to build community through education, Jonathan, Rina, and Eric implicitly address the implications of the dynamic relationship between the concepts of agency and communion. The psychologist David Bakan first drew attention to the terms in his book *The Duality of Human Existence* (1966). According to Bakan, they describe "two fundamental modalities of human existence. Agency refers to an individual's striving to master the environment, to assert the self, to experience competence, achievement, and power. In contrast, communion refers to a person's desire to closely relate to and cooperate and merge with others" (Diehl et al. 2008, para. 2). Plentiful psychological research into agency and communion has generated valuable discoveries about adult development over the lifespan. But little attention has been given to it in scholarship on adult education, adult religious education, faith development, or adult Jewish learning. Why this is so is unclear, especially given the emphasis on developmental concerns in these fields. As rabbis for whom building community is closely tied to educational processes, the centrality of how agency and communion function in their learners' lives would be a valuable contribution to our understanding of how clergy work with adults. How does adult learning inform and transform an adult's agency and communion in relation to a religious tradition? How do the stories they hear and those they tell about themselves affect their adult faith development? How does the tension between agency and communion shape their commitments to their religious communities? All of these areas await further research about rabbis and their adult learners.

The Constellation

To forge community requires an ability to inspire loyalty. We live in an era when many adults find that their time and energy are constantly expended in a seemingly endless number of directions. Given that reality, how does a congregation create attachments that are vital enough to be felt as loyalties? As leaders of their congregations, the processes by which clergy commit themselves to this task formatively shape the spirit of their institutions. To define one's mission as a religious leader so that teaching and learning are at the heart of constructing community speaks to an abiding faith in the present generation's ability to invigorate a faith tradition. It expresses a conviction that learning together is a primary pathway towards sustaining that tradition's vibrancy.

Through learning, the past and present are explored together so that their multilayered meanings become embedded in our collective consciousness. Whether we study the narratives in our sacred books or tell each other our own, these stories help foster the connections and coherence that lie at the heart of any vibrant congregational identity. Moreover, when rabbis build community through education with their congregant-learners, the potential for transformation reaches beyond the current generation. It affirms the potential for a religious tradition to constantly renew itself as a vital force rather than as a static relic of the past. In this way it becomes a "living tradition" (Hansen 2001, 116).

The educational philosopher David Hansen has written, " . . . a sense of tradition encourages a teacher to see her- or himself as being in time, as a person responsible for ensuring that things of value—knowledge, understanding, outlooks—endure in a dynamic way for future generations" (2001, 115). As synagogue community builders, Jonathan, Rina, and Eric invite their adult learners to discover that they too can embody the qualities that Hansen identifies as fundamental to a teacher's sense of transcendent purpose. A pursuit of this kind reaches back in time towards the heart of God's call to the recently freed Israelite slaves as described in the book of Exodus: "And let them make me a sanctuary that I may dwell among them" (25:7). And, just as crucially, it reaches forward into the future, as expressed in a rabbinic commentary that imagines God eternally instructing the people of Israel, "Wherever you travel, build a shrine for me that I may dwell among you" (*Exodus Rabbah* 33:1).

COMMUNITY BUILDER CHECKLIST

- How do I understand the term "community" within my synagogue?
- How do I support community building through adult education?
- In what ways do I (or might I) collaborate with colleagues and laity to foster community through adult education?
- How can teaching adults with stories support community building?
- How can adult learning empower participants to take an active role in communal life?

chapter 8

A CLERGY FOR OUR TIME

Discussion is not a mere means to an end but constitutes an enactment of significant values of listening, articulating, respecting others, and sustaining human community. —HANSEN 2011, 25

A major impetus behind this book's conception was a wish to promote thoughtful discussion about clergy identity and practice in the United States at the start of the twenty-first century. In his book *Exploring the Moral Heart of Teaching: Toward a Teacher's Creed*, educational philosopher David Hansen described teaching as "a longstanding human endeavor that has a distinctive identity and a distinctive contribution to make to human flourishing" (2001, x). Rabbis Jonathan Fisk, Rina Lewin, and Eric Miller invite us to contemplate Hansen's claim in light of religious education and faith formation. Their portraits challenge us to discuss the various educational dispositions clergy require in order to cultivate their identity as teachers. In a dizzyingly complex world, these rabbis offer us compelling ways to imagine adult education as the key to a coherent and dynamic religious life. That is in and of itself a significant accomplishment. In the process, they and their learners contribute to creating communities infused with an enduring awareness of the sacred in our lives.

Over the course of research, I became increasingly convinced that clergy continue to matter to our society. The openness and vibrancy I encountered in the three rabbis and in their congregations filled me with hope. The rich frequency of the face-to-face relationships that they supported struck me as verging on revolutionary, given that our culture seems to be catapulting itself in the opposite direction. Yet even as their examples

149

gave me confidence, I became aware of the extent to which American adults no longer turn reflexively to their clergy or to their places of worship in their quest for community, meaning, or comfort. I grasped just how real is the possibility of clergy and congregational communities becoming increasingly marginal to our society. This final chapter addresses the ways that rabbis and other members of the American clergy can reverse the drift towards irrelevance. The first part of the chapter suggests concrete recommendations for practice. The second returns to the constellation of narrative, transformation, and spirituality to argue why it matters so urgently.

CLERGY PRACTICES

Judaism affirms the power of learning to redeem an imperfect world. Other faith traditions do so as well. As teachers, contemporary clergy will find that when adult education in our congregations encourages learners to share their questions, concerns, doubts, beliefs, and values it forges beneficial connections of all kinds. To use the vocabulary of faith, it sets in motion a redemptive process. To help do so, however, requires preparation and practice. It can be learned, which is why research that is shared with seminaries and clergy alike is valuable. In the spirit of portraiture, such scholarship intentionally aims to build bridges with practitioners. It gears its discoveries towards conversation among those who rarely communicate with each other about these matters. Clergy cannot do the work we see happening in this book in isolation. As the portraits reveal, clergy need to study with one another regularly. They require time to reflect on their teaching with each other. Discussions among seminary faculty, seminary students, and clergy in congregations (across denominations and among different religious traditions) about teaching and learning need to occur consistently. Ongoing dialogue across boundaries and borders, whether intercongregational, interdenominational, or interreligious, is essential.

The rabbis portrayed here define their rabbinates in the context of teaching and learning. They purposefully promote, support, and cultivate education as a primary value and activity in their synagogues. Furthermore, because they prioritize teaching as the core of their rabbinic identities, they work to establish communities that self-consciously define themselves as learning congregations. The rabbi's explicit articulation in word and deed of the centrality of education influences the congregation's narrative. Over time a mutuality of purpose develops between the rabbi's perception and the congregation's vision of itself as a community of learners. My research suggests, moreover, that congregational rabbis, and by extension clergy of other faiths, hold a uniquely influential position with regard to teaching adults for the following reasons:

- Even in today's environment of fluid loyalties, synagogues and churches remain among the most important institutions in American religious life. Clergy are sometimes the first and often the only teachers that adult learners encounter in these settings.

- Clergy often come to know their congregants and the families over a life span, both within and outside the learning setting. This vantage point gives them a unique opportunity to understand more fully the range of concerns and questions that adults bring to their learning.

- Clergy are main movers in helping to foster connections to the broader congregational community. They lead the way in developing bonds and loyalties that extend beyond any specific course or particular experience. As such, clergy who guide their congregants through teaching and learning nourish communal vitality through education.

- Clergy have the authority to promote learning in settings that overcome the all too common distinction between formal and informal approaches to education. They would benefit by deliberating about how to incorporate this synthesis intentionally as part of a broader expression of the relationship between community and learning. The descriptions of the annual retreat at Rina's synagogue and of Jonathan's trips to Israel with his congregants (and, as of 2014, with Temple Sinai and a neighboring church together) are but two examples of this kind of integration. More innovative experimentation is urgently needed in this area.

These understandings of the clergy's role put the emphasis on the interpersonal connection between them and their congregants. Relationships are at the heart of the adult learning enterprise. While clergy may feel driven to communicate their knowledge of tradition, relationships are the essential soil out of which this knowledge comes alive for many of their learners. The richer the soil is the more abundant the garden will be. Seminaries need to prepare their students for this central aspect of their work in a coherent way. Their curriculum must reflect the priority of interpersonal relationships in an intentional manner, rather than in an ad hoc or incidental one.

Seminary Preparation

Of the three rabbis portrayed in this book, only Jonathan held an advanced degree in Jewish education. Eric explicitly stated that he had never taken any education courses. Nor had he done any independent reading related to educational practice or theory. Rina emphasized how she learned about teaching primarily from the positions she held before attending rabbinical school. Her husband's recommendations helped her understand how to best teach adults.

On the one hand, these three rabbis appear to have learned about teaching, and teaching adults in particular, primarily through the "apprenticeship of observation" (Lortie 1975). During their rabbinates, they have figured out what to do well through trial and error. On the other hand, this description simplifies the picture of their paths towards excellence. Rina and Eric both pursued prior careers that spanned almost two decades as Jewish educators before becoming congregational rabbis. All three rabbis are highly self-reflective individuals who continually pay attention to how they can evaluate their teaching. We cannot be certain that either situation is the case with other rabbis, especially those who are in the early years of the rabbinate. My research suggests that rabbinical students, as well as those studying for the clergy in seminaries beyond the Jewish world, would benefit by opportunities for more comprehensive exploration of their own identities as teachers, and of the practice of educating adults, while attending seminary. A firmer understanding of adult development is vital to this trajectory.

When seminaries envision their students' identities as teachers, they would do well to think especially attentively about the relationship between teaching and community building. Over a decade ago Jewish educational scholar Jeffrey Schein proposed that rabbinical seminaries needed to consider the kinds of teaching methods their faculties used, no less than how they conceptualized learning. He wrote, "Rabbis as teachers are shaped as much by the way they are taught in seminary as by any explicit theory of how they, as future rabbis, might communicate Jewish knowledge" (1998, 16). Foster and his colleagues argued similarly for clergy more generally in *Educating Clergy: Teaching Practices and Pastoral Imagination* (2005).

Teachers who work in all kinds of educational institutions find that many of our schools are rapidly making changes that lead to the incorporation of new Internet-driven technologies into curricula, courses, and teaching. The changes raise a welter of questions about how to teach. They form part of a larger discussion about the means and purposes of education, and higher education in particular, more broadly in American society. Seminaries are part of this revolution. Now is a particularly apt juncture for seminaries to keep in mind that the way students are taught is very often exactly how they go on to teach others. What do our teaching practices model for soon-to-be-clergy? Now is a perfect occasion for seminary leaders and faculty to study carefully the influence on their students of their teaching practice, including not only online forms of education, but also, and crucially, face-to-face encounters. How do approaches to teaching embedded in a seminary's culture undermine or support the kinds of interactions clergy need to have with congregants when they join congregations as communal leaders and religious educators?

The Imperative of Ongoing Learning

When they leave their seminaries, rabbis may find that opportunities to learn with colleagues evaporate. Yet Jonathan, Rina, and Eric continue to view themselves as learners. To all three of them studying is crucial to their success as teachers. Remaining learners is essential to their authenticity as rabbinic educators. They individually stressed the imperative of studying in the company of rabbinic colleagues. Congregations must support this kind of ongoing learning for their clergy. Clergy should be allowed time away from their congregations for sustained periods of collegial study and reflection. Retreats and conferences are but two examples of these kinds of opportunities. Others await creation, such as the weekly rabbinic learning among clergy that Eric and Rina do with colleagues in their town.

THE CONSTELLATION OF NARRATIVE, TRANSFORMATION, AND SPIRITUALITY

In the introductory chapter I mentioned that this book's genesis could be traced to my first foray into portraiture as an advanced graduate student at the Jewish Theological Seminary. The subject of that effort was Rabbi Neil Gillman, who at the time was the Aaron Rabinowitz and Simon H. Rifkind Professor of Jewish Thought. Rabbi Gillman was a teacher who became a generous mentor to me. In his long tenure at the Seminary he mentored several generations of rabbinical students in his capacity as a professor, rabbi, and dean of the rabbinical school. Although I was not studying for the rabbinate, my exposure to Rabbi Gillman's teaching helped set me upon the path that eventually became this book.

Rabbi Gillman was not a congregational rabbi. Yet in his later years as a professor he chose to dedicate a significant amount of time to teaching adults in synagogues. Our conversations impressed upon me how necessary it was for seminary educators to engage with adult learners beyond the academy. In our many absorbing discussions, both those that led to my article about his teaching and others, he shared with me his high regard for the adults he encountered in these settings. He was as far from the cloistered scholar who distanced himself from the untutored masses as any philosopher could be. On the contrary, he found his interactions with laypeople bracing and provocative. As a theologian, he learned from them about the dilemmas they had regarding God. He discovered that they rarely discussed these issues with their rabbis. In response to this realization, he decided to transform his teaching of rabbinical students into one that emphasized personal theology rather than academically dispassionate inquiry. He pushed his seminarians to articulate orally and in writing their theologies on a range of crucial subjects. To him theology was at its core an arena for existential inquiry. As his student I can attest to the transformative effect of that approach on my faith commitments as a Jew and as a human being. My adult understanding of God emerged as a result of his teaching influence.

Put differently, Rabbi Gillman concerned himself with his learners as much as he did with his subject matter. A rabbi's task as a teacher is to address the whole person. Jonathan, Rina, and Eric corroborated what I heard initially articulated in my exchanges with Rabbi Gillman. Over the trajectory of this book, reference to how adults evolve during the course of their lives has been a constant refrain. Adult development theory has been and remains a focus of scholarly research in adult education, even as how it is understood has taken on new dimensions. Narrative identity, spiritual formation, and gender studies, for example, reflect the ongoing evolution of adult developmental theories. As Laurent Daloz pointed out in his book *Mentor*, " . . . *development* is more than simply change. Moreover, development seems to happen not in a gradual and linear way but in distinct and recognizable leaps—in a series of spiraling plateaus rather than a smooth slope" (1999, 23). In their relationships with adult learners, clergy must attend to the spiraling pattern observed by Daloz.

A Clergy for Our Time

As I reread the portraits in preparation to write this final chapter, I noted how infrequently the rabbis mentioned God in our interviews. They comfortably spoke about faith, belief, tradition, ritual, and spirituality. God came up, but only appeared intermittently as a focal point. Yet, even many years after my interviews and observations I remember feeling that God's presence—imagined by me as an abundant source of care and wisdom—accompanied them in their teaching. This experience is admittedly entirely subjective. I cannot offer a satisfactory answer to the paradox described here. Perhaps as a researcher I did not directly question them about God. Maybe they are less explicit in their references to God when they teach, as Rabbi Gillman had heard from his adult learners about other rabbis. In this regard, spiritual formation and faith development are primary areas for further inquiry into the role of clergy as teachers of adults. These are domains that transcend particular religious traditions and religion in general as a subject.

One way to further this understanding is through the constellation of narrative, transformation, and spirituality. I am struck by the metaphor of a constellation because of its resonance with one of the foundational images that appear in the canonical sources of many faiths: the vision of a God who resides in the Heavens. By extension, God's presence, however we understand it, can be expressed in the constellation that illuminates Jonathan, Rina, and Eric's work as teachers. Exploring the constellation can lead to an array of discussions about the intersection of education, faith, and God among clergy, among seminary faculty, between seminary educators and their students, and across the divide that all too often separates seminary academics from clergy in congregations. These intentional conversations also need to be supported by clergy in their congregations. Other educators who work with adults would benefit by inclusion in such discussions. Further research by scholars will deepen our understanding of the processes and outcomes that constitute the constellation.

Narratives heard, told, read, remembered, and reflected on together invite teacher and learner to situate their experiences within a framework that is wide and deep. They allow for the past—distant and recent, mythic and historical—to converse with the present. Stories, according to McAdams,

> ... help us organize our thoughts, providing a narrative for human intentions and interpersonal events that is readily remembered and told. In some instances, stories may also mend us when

155

> we are broken, heal us when we are sick, and even move us toward psychological fulfillment and maturity. (1993, 31)

From this perspective, narrative contains within it a movement towards transformation. The narrative learning that happens when Jonathan, Rina, and Eric teach gives their learners a chance to discover connections and patterns in their lives. They link rabbi and learners with a tradition, a faith and, crucially, with one another.

Transformation is an internal process that takes place in the life of an individual. It becomes communal when a group of learners contributes its distinctive character to a community's unfolding story. Just as people change, so do communities and the traditions to which they are loyal. Where there is intentionality in this process, the direction it moves us towards is wisdom, and towards the wholeness that the root of the Hebrew word for peace— shalom—connotes. At its core, then, this kind of transformation joins the project for a healed world—for a redeemed world—rather than a fractured and broken one. As befits a clergy living in a post-modern universe, Jonathan, Rina, and Eric reject absolute truths for human beings. Yet again and again they trust that transformative learning is at its core redemptive. It is thus profoundly bound up with the deepest spiritual yearnings of human beings for wholeness.

In 1934 the philosopher Martin Buber delivered a talk at the Frankfurt Lehrhaus. The Lehrhaus was the renowned center for adult Jewish education in Frankfurt, Germany, founded in 1920. Buber helped sustain its mission throughout the 1930s, before his departure for Jerusalem in 1938. At that tragic period in German Jewry, facing an abyss to come that few could even imagine, Buber called his address "Teaching and Deed." In it, he discussed the intertwined relationship of teaching, learning, and living. In Buber's words:

> The life of the spirit of a people is renewed whenever a teaching generation transmits it to a learning generation which, in turn—as learners grow into teachers—transmits the spirit through the lips of new teachers to the ears of new pupils; yet this process of education involves the person as a whole . . . Here, if anywhere, it is impossible to teach or to learn without living. The teachings must not be treated as a collection of knowable material; they resist such treatment. Either the teachings live in the life of a responsible human, or they are not alive at all . . . (2002, 234–6)

Buber, drawing on birth metaphors, outlines how a faith tradition, in this instance Judaism, finds its present purpose through each generation's commitment to its renewal. Teaching of the kind that Buber describes reveals the spirit that ultimately binds all creation together. This spirit resides in each of us and between us. Echoing Rabbi Eric Miller's understanding of Torah, through teaching and learning we encounter that spirit as a living force, and in so doing discover "the deeper meaning of why we're here."

Appendix A

CONSENT LETTER

Sarah Tauber
125 Central Avenue, Apt. B7
Rye, New York 10580

Dear Rabbi_____,

I am writing a dissertation in Jewish education at the Jewish Theological Seminary of America on the role of the congregational rabbi as a teacher of adults using the qualitative research method known as portraiture. The purpose of the research is to learn more about congregational rabbis' perception and practice as teachers of adults.

I would like to interview you and observe your teaching as part of my research. There will be no compensation for your participation. You may discontinue participation at any time.

I will give you a fictitious name in the dissertation and eliminate or give a fictitious name to any institution to which you refer. I will be happy to share my research with you for your feedback. If you have any questions about this research project or would like more information before, during, or after the study, you may contact my adviser, Dr. Carol Ingall, at caingall@jtsa.edu. I hope that you will agree to work with me on this project.

APPENDIX A: CONSENT LETTER

Sincerely,

Sarah Tauber

I have been informed of the goals and rationale of the dissertation project and consent to participating in it.

Date_____

Participant's Signature_____

Appendix B

OPEN ENDED SEMI-STRUCTURED INTERVIEW QUESTIONS

Interview One: The work of the rabbi

Tell me about yourself as a congregational rabbi

Tell me about the place teaching holds in your rabbinate

Tell me about your approach to teaching adults

Interview Two: Biography

Tell me about your family

Tell me about your Jewish education prior to rabbinical school

When did you decide to become a rabbi?

Why did you decide to become a rabbi?

Interview Three: Reflection

When do you feel most like a rabbi?

Who are your role models and why are they models?

What have you learned about teaching adults as a rabbi?

What does the phrase "teaching Torah" mean to you?

APPENDIX B: INTERVIEW QUESTIONS

Possible additional questions if necessary:

What do you think adult learners care most about in their rabbi as a teacher?

What motivates adults to learn with you?

BIBLIOGRAPHY

Aberbach, Moshe. 1967. "The Relations Between Master and Disciple in the Talmudic Age." In *Essays Presented To Israel Brodie Chief Rabbi*, edited by H. J. Zimmels, et al., 1–24. London: Soncino.
Abrahams, Israel, et al. 2007. "Belief." In *Encyclopaedia Judaica*, edited by Michael Berenbaum and Fred Skolnik, 3:290–94. Detroit, MI: Macmillan.
Apps, Jerold W. 1991. *Mastering the Teaching of Adults*. Malabar: Krieger.
Argyis, Chris, and Donald A. Schoen. 1974. *Theory in Practice: Increasing Professional Effectiveness*. San Francisco: Jossey-Bass.
Aron, Isa. 2000. *Becoming a Congregation of Learners: Learning as a Key to Revitalizing Congregational Life*. Woodstock, VT: Jewish Lights.
Aron, Isa, et al. 1995. *A Congregation of Learners: Transforming the Synagogue into a Learning Community*. New York: UAHC.
Aron, Isa, and Diane T. Schuster. 1998. "Extending the Chain of Tradition: Reflections on the Goals of Adult Text Study." *Journal of Jewish Education* 64:44–56.
Bakan, David. 1966. *The Duality of Human Existence: Isolation and Communion in Western Man*. Boston: Beacon.
Belenky, Mary F., et al. 1986. *Women's Ways of Knowing: The Development of Self, Voice, and Mind*. New York: Basic.
Biemann, Asher D., ed. 2002. *The Martin Buber Reader: Essential Writings*. New York: Palgrave Macmillan.
Bloom, Jack H. 1976. "The Rabbi as Symbolic Exemplar." PhD diss., Columbia University.
Brookfield, Stephen D. 1986. *Understanding and Facilitating Adult Learning: A Comprehensive Analysis of Principles and Effective Practices*. San Francisco: Jossey-Bass.
———. 1991. "Discussion." In *Adult Learning Methods: A Guide for Effective Instruction*, edited by Michael W. Galbraith, 187–204. Malabar, FL: Krieger.
———. 2006. *The Skillful Teacher: On Technique, Trust, and Responsiveness in the Classroom*. San Francisco: Jossey-Bass.
Brookfield, Stephen D., and Stephen Preskill. 2005. *Discussion as a Way of Teaching: Tools and Techniques for Democratic Classrooms*. 2nd ed. San Francisco: Jossey-Bass.
Brown, George Jr. "Dwayne Huebner." *Talbot School of Theology*. http://www.talbot.edu/ce20/educators/protestant/dwayne_huebner/.
Buber, Martin. 2002. "Teaching and Deed." In *The Martin Buber Reader: Essential Writings*, edited by Asher D. Biemann, 234–39. New York: Palgrave Macmillan.

Bibliography

Bycel, Lee T. 1995. "The Transformation of the Rabbi's Role: Curricular Implications." Masters Thesis, Claremont School of Theology.

Caffarela, Rosemary S., and Carolyn M. Clark. 1999. "Development and Learning: Themes and Conclusions." *New Directions for Adult and Continuing Education* 84:97–100.

Carey, Benedict. 2007. "This is Your Life (and How You Tell It)." *New York Times*, May 22. http://nytimes.com/2007/05/22/health/psychology/22narr.html.

Chamberlin, Judi. 2013. "A Working Definition of Empowerment." *National Empowerment Center*. http://www.power2u.org/articles/empower/working_def.html.

Charmaz, Kathy. 2006. *Constructing Grounded Theory: A Practical Guide Through Qualitative Analysis*. London: Sage.

Clark, Carolyn M., and Marsha Rossiter. 2008. "Narrative Learning in Adulthood." *New Directions for Adult and Continuing Education* 119:61–70.

Cohen, Steven M., and Aryeh Davidson. 2001. *Adult Jewish Learning in America: Current Patterns and Prospects for Growth*. New York: JCCA and the Jewish Theological Seminary.

Conti, Gary J. 1991. "Identifying Your Teaching Style." In *Adult Learning Methods: A Guide for Effective Instruction*, edited by Michael W. Galbraith, 79–96. Malabar: Krieger.

Corradetti, Claudio. "The Frankfurt School and Critical Theory." *Internet Encyclopedia of Philosophy*. http://iep.utm.edu/frankfur/.

Cranton, Patricia. 1996. *Professional Development and Transformative Learning: New Perspectives for Teachers of Adults*. San Francisco: Jossey-Bass.

———. 2006. "Integrating Perspectives on Authenticity." *New Directions for Adult and Continuing Education* 111:83–88.

———. 2006a. "Teaching for Transformation." *New Directions for Adult and Continuing Education* 93:63–72.

Cranton, Patricia, and Edward W. Taylor. 2012. "Transformative Learning Theory: Seeking a More Unified Theory." In *The Handbook of Transformative Learning: Theory, Research, and Practice*, edited by Edward W. Taylor, et al., 3–20. San Francisco: Jossey-Bass.

Daloz, Laurent A. 1999. *Mentor: Guiding the Journey of Adult Learners*. 2nd ed. San Francisco: Jossey-Bass.

Deshler, David, and Nancy Hagan. 1989. "Adult Education Research: Issues and Directions." In *Handbook of Adult and Continuing Education*, edited by Sharan B. Merriam and Phyllis M. Cunningham, 147–67. San Francisco: Jossey-Bass.

Diehl, Manfred, et al. 2004. "Agency and Communion Attributes in Adults' Spontaneous Self-Representation." *International Journal of Behavior Development* 28:1–15. http://www.ncbi.him.nih.gov/pmc/articles/PMC2441921.

Dirkx, John M. 2006. "Authenticity and Imagination." *New Directions for Adult and Continuing Education* 111:27–40.

Dykstra, Craig, and Sharon Parks, eds. 1986. *Faith Development and Fowler*. Birmingham, AL: Religious Education.

Elias, John D. 1993. *The Foundations of Religious Education*. 2nd ed. Malabar: Krieger.

Elias, John D., and Sharan B. Merriam. 1980. *Philosophical Foundations of Adult Education*. Malabar, FL: Krieger.

English, Leona M., and Marie A. Gillen. 2000. "Editor's Notes." *New Directions for Adult and Continuing Education* 85:1–5.

Farrah, Shirley J. 1991. "Lecture." In *Adult Learning Methods: A Guide for Effective Instruction*, edited by Michael W. Galbraith, 161–86. Malabar, FL: Krieger.

BIBLIOGRAPHY

Flannery, Danielle D., and Elizabeth Hayes. 2001. "Challenging Adult Learning: A Feminist Perspective." In *Making Space: Merging Theory and Practice in Adult Education*, edited by Vanessa Sheared and Peggy A. Sissel, 29–41. Westport, CT: Bergin and Garvey.

Flexner, Paul. 1995. "Facilitating Adult Jewish Learning." PhD diss., Teachers College.

Foltz, Nancy T., ed. 1986. *Handbook of Adult Religious Education*. Birmingham, AL: Religious Education.

Foster, Charles R., et al. 2006. *Educating Clergy: Teaching Practices and Pastoral Imagination*. San Francisco: Jossey-Bass.

Fowler, James W. 1981. *Stages of Faith: The Psychology of Human Development and the Quest for Meaning*. New York: Harper Collins.

Freire, Paolo. 1972. *Pedagogy of the Oppressed*. New York: Herder and Herder.

Fried, Stephen. 2002. *The New Rabbi*. New York: Bantam.

Glaser, Barney, and Anselm Strauss. 1967. *The Discovery of Grounded Theory*. Chicago: Aldine.

Goldin, Hyman, E., trans. 1962. *Ethics of the Fathers*. New York: Hebrew.

Golemon, Larry A., ed. 2010. *Living Our Story: Narrative Leadership and Congregational Culture*. Herndon, VA: Alban Institute.

Grant, Lisa D. 2008. "Authenticity, Autonomy, and Authority: Feminist Jewish Learning Among Post-Soviet Women." *Journal of Jewish Education* 74.1:83–102.

Grant, Lisa D., and Diane Tickton Schuster. 2011. "Adult Jewish Learning: The Landscape." In *International Handbook of Jewish Education*, edited by Helena Miler, et al., 669–89. London: Springer.

Grant, Lisa D., et al. 2004. *A Journey of Heart and Mind: Transformative Jewish Learning in Adulthood*. New York: JTS.

Grasha, Anthony A. 1996. *Teaching with Style*. San Bernadino, CA: Alliance.

Grossman, Pamela L. 1991. "What Are We Talking About Anyhow? Subject-Matter Knowledge of English Teachers." In *Advances in Research on Teaching*, Vol. 2, edited by Jere Brophy, 245–64. New York: JAI.

Gudmundsdottir, Sigrun. 1995. "The Narrative Nature of Pedagogical Content Knowledge." In *Narrative in Teaching, Learning, and Research*, edited by Hunter McKewan and Kieran Egan, 24–38. New York: Teachers College Press.

Hansen, David T. 2001. *Exploring the Moral Heart of Teaching: Towards a Teacher's Creed*. New York: Teachers College Press.

Harris, Maria. 1987. *Teaching and Religious Imagination: An Essay in the Theology of Teaching*. San Francisco: Harper.

———. 1988. *Women and Teaching*. Mahwah, NJ: Paulist.

Hayes, Elizabeth, and Danielle D. Flannery. 2000. *Women as Learners: The Significance of Gender in Adult Learning*. San Francisco: Jossey-Bass.

Heimlich, Joe E., and Emmalou Norland. 2002. "Teaching Style: Where are We Now?" *New Directions for Adult and Continuing Education* 93:17–26.

Hester, Richard L., and Kelli Walker-Jones. 2009. *Know Your Story and Lead with It: The Power of Narrative in Clergy Leadership*. Herndon: Alban Institute.

Holtz, Barry W. 2003. *Textual Knowledge: Teaching the Bible in Theory and Practice*. New York: JTS.

Holzer, Elie, and Orit Kent. 2013. *A Philosophy of Havruta: Understanding and Teaching the Art of Text Study in Pairs*. Boston: Academic Studies.

Bibliography

Huebner, Dwayne E. 1999. *The Lure of the Transcendent: Collected Essays by Dwayne E. Huebner*. Mahwah, NJ: Lawrence Erlbaum.

Imel, Susan. 1989. "The Field Literature and Information Source." In *Handbook of Adult and Continuing Education*, edited by Sharan B. Merriam and Phyllis M. Cunningham. 134–46. San Francisco: Jossey-Bass.

Jewish Publication Society. 1999. *JPS Hebrew English Tanakh*. 2nd ed. Philadephia: Jewish Publication Society.

Kegan, Robert. 1982. *The Evolving Self: Problem and Process in Human Development*. Cambridge: Harvard University Press.

———. 1994. *In Over Our Heads: The Mental Demands of Modern Life*. Cambridge: Harvard University Press.

———. 2000. "What "Form" Transforms? A Constructive-Developmental Approach to Transformative Learning." In *Learning as Transformation: Critical Perspectives on a Theory in Progress*, edited by Jack Mezirow, 35–69. San Francisco: Jossey-Bass.

Kimelman, Reuven. 1987. "Leadership and Community in Judaism." *Tikkun* 2.5, 26–30, 88–91.

Knowles, M. S. 1980. *The Modern Practice of Adult Education: From Pedagoy to Andragogy*, Revised and Updated. Chicago: Follett.

———. 1984. *The Adult Learner: A Neglected Species*. 3rd ed. Houston, TX: Gulf.

Kress, Jeff S., et al. 2007. "Perceptions and Roles of Conservative Rabbis: Findings and Implications Related to Identity and Education." *Journal of Jewish Education* 73.3:191–208.

Lawrence-Lightfoot, Sara. 1983. *The Good High School: Portraits of Character and Culture*. New York: Basic.

Lawrence-Lightfoot, Sara, and Jessica Hoffman Davis. 1997. *The Art and Science of Portraiture*. San Francisco: Jossey-Bass.

Lortie, Dan C. 1977. *Schoolteacher: A Sociological Study*. New York: University of Chicago Press.

Maslow, Abraham H. 1970. *Motivation and Personality*. 2nd ed. New York: Harper and Row.

McAdams, Dan P. 1993. *The Stories We Live By: Personal Myths and the Making of the Self*. New York: Guilford.

———. 2001. "The Psychology of Life Stories." *Review of General Psychology* 5:100–22.

———. 2005. *The Redemptive Self: Stories Americans Live By*. Oxford: Oxford University Press.

Marcus, Jacob R., and Abraham J. Peck. 1985. *The American Rabbinate: A Century of Continuity and Change*. Hoboken, NJ: KTAV.

McKenzie, Leon. 1982. *The Religious Education of Adults*. Birmingham, AL: Religious Education.

Merriam, Sharan B. 2009. *Qualitative Research: A Guide to Design and Implementation*. San Francisco: Jossey-Bass.

Merriam, Sharan B., et al. 2007. *Learning In Adulthood: A Comprehensive Guide*. San Francisco: Jossey-Bass.

Merriam, Sharan B., and Ralph G. Brockett. 1997. *The Profession and Practice of Adult Education*: An Introduction. San Francisco: Jossey-Bass.

Mezirow, Jack. 1990. "How Critical Reflection Triggers Transformational Learning." In *Fostering Critical Reflection in Adulthood: A Guide to Transformative and Emancipatory Learning*, edited by Jack Mezirow, 1–21. San Francisco: Jossey-Bass.

———. 1991. *Transformative Dimensions of Adult Learning.* San Francisco: Jossey-Bass.

———. 2000. "Learning to Think Like an Adult." In *Learning as Transformation: Critical Perspectives on a Theory in Progress,* edited by Jack Mezirow, 3–33. San Francisco: Jossey-Bass.

Moore, Mary E. Mullino. 1998. *Teaching from the Heart: Theology and Educational Method.* Harrisburg, PA: Trinity.

Palmer, Parker J. 1998. *The Courage to Teach: Exploring the Inner Landscape of a Teacher's Life.* San Francisco: Jossey-Bass.

Parks, Sharon Daloz. 1991. *The Critical Years: Young Adults and The Search for Meaning, Faith, and Commitment.* New York: Harper Collins.

———. 2011. *Big Questions, Worthy Dreams: Mentoring Emerging Adults in Their Search for Meaning, Purpose, and Faith.* San Francisco: Jossey-Bass.

Peruniak, Geoff. "Laurent Daloz: Helping Adults Learning: Mentoring and the Definition of a Good Education." *Aurora.* 1990. http://aurora.icaap.org/index.php/aurora/article/view/39/50.

Pratt, Daniel D. 1993. "Andragogy After Twenty Five Years." *New Directions for Adult and Continuing Education* 57:15–24.

Polkinghorne, Donald E. 1988. *Narrative Knowing and the Human Sciences.* Albany, NY: SUNY Press.

Randall, William. 1996. "Restorying a Life: Adult Education and Transformative Learning." In *Aging and Biography: Explorations in Adult Development,* edited by James E. Birren, et al., 225–47. New York: Springer.

Reeves, Patricia M. 1990. "Psychological Development: Becoming a Person." *New Directions for Adult and Continuing Education* 84:19–28.

Rogers, Carl. 1969. *Freedom to Learn.* Columbus, OH: Merrill.

Rosenak, Michael. 1987. *Commandments and Concerns: Jewish Religious Education in Secular Society.* New York: JPS.

Rossiter, Marsha. 1999. "Understanding Adult Development as Narrative." *New Directions for Adult and Continuing Education* 84:77–86.

———. 1999a. "A Narrative Approach to Development: Implications for Adult Education." *Adult Education Quarterly* 50:56–71.

———. 2002. "Narrative and Stories in Adult Teaching and Learning." *ERIC Digest.* http://files.eric.ed.gov/fulltext/ED473147.pdf.

Rossiter, Marsha, and M. Carolyn Clark. 2007. *Narrative and the Practice of Adult Education.* Malabar, FL: Krieger.

Rowell, J. C. 2000. "Empowering Images of the Minister as Teacher." *Religious Education* 95:64–78.

Schein, Jeffrey L. 1988. "Rabbi as Teacher: The Process of Formulating Educational Goals for Jewish Leadership." *Journal of Jewish Education* 2:15–17.

Schoen, Donald A. 1983. *The Reflective Practitioner: How Professionals Think in Action.* New York: Basic.

———. 1987. *Educating the Reflective Practitioner: Toward a New Design for Teaching and Learning in the Professions.* San Francisco: Jossey-Bass.

Schorsch, Ismar. 1990-1991. "The Modern Rabbinate—Then and Now." *Conservative Judaism* 43:12–20.

Schultz, Rachel Gelfman. "Havruta: Learning in Pairs." *My Jewish Learning.* http://www.myjewishlearning.com/practices/Ritual/Torah_Study/How_to_Study_Torah/Havruta_Learning_in_Pairs_.shtml.

Bibliography

Schuster, Diane T. 2003. *Jewish Lives, Jewish Learning: Adult Jewish Learning in Theory and Practice.* New York: UAHC.

———. 2003a. "Teaching Jewish Adults." In *The Ultimate Jewish Teacher's Handbook,* edited by Nehama Moskowitz, 140–63. Denver, CO: ARE.

———. 2005. "Adult Jewish Learners: Entering the Conversation." *Journal of Jewish Education* 71:245–47.

Schuster, Diane T, and Lisa D. Grant. 2005. "Adult Jewish Learning: What Do We Know? What Do We Need to Know?" *Journal of Jewish Education* 71:179–200.

Sigel, Irving E., et al. 2007. "Beyond Questioning: Inquiry Strategies and Cognitive and Affective Elements of Jewish Education." *Journal of Jewish Education* 73:51–66.

Smith, Mark K. 1996; 1999; 2010. "Andragogy." *Encyclopaedia of Informal Education.* http://www.infed.org/mobi/andragogy.

Steinsalz, Adin, ed. 1989. *The Talmud. Steinsaltz Edition.* New York: Random House.

Tauber, Sarah. 2013. "The Midwife: Portrait of a Congregational Rabbi as a Teacher of Adults." *Journal of Jewish Education* 79.1:24–48.

———. 2013a. "Teaching Through Personal Stories: Congregational Rabbis and Teaching Adults." *Journal of Jewish Education* 79.4:432–52.

Taylor, Edward W., and M. J. Snyder. 2012. "A Critical Review of Research on Transformative Learning Theory." In *The Handbook of Transformative Learning Theory: Theory, Research, and Practice,* edited by Edward W. Taylor and Patricia Cranton, 37–55. San Francisco: Jossey-Bass.

Taylor, Edward W., et al. 2012. *The Handbook of Transformative Learning: Theory, Research, and Practice.* San Francisco: Jossey-Bass.

Tennant, Mark. 2005. *Psychology and Adult Learning.* 3rd ed. New York: Routledge.

Tisdell, E. 2008. "Spirituality and Adult Learning." *New Directions for Adult and Continuing Education* 119:27–36.

Vella, Jane. 2000. *Taking Learning to Task: Creative Strategies for Teaching Adults.* San Francisco: Jossey-Bass.

———. 2002. *Learning to Listen, Learning to Teach: The Power of Dialogue in Educating Adults.* San Francisco: Jossey-Bass.

———. 2007. *On Teaching and Learning: Putting the Principles of Dialogue Education into Action.* San Francisco: Jossey-Bass.

Vogel, Linda J. 1999. *Teaching in Communities of Faith.* San Francisco: Jossey-Bass.

Wertheimer, Jack. 2005. "The American Synagogue: Recent Issues and Trend." *American Jewish Yearbook* 105:3–83.

Wickett, R. E. Y. 1991. *Modes of Adult Religious Education Practice.* Birmingham, AL: Religious Education.

Wilkes, Paul. 1994. *And They Shall Be My People: An American Rabbi and His Congregation.* New York: Grove.

Woocher, Jonathan. 1995. "Toward a 'Unified Field Theory' of Jewish Continuity." In *A Congregation of Learners: Transforming the Synagogue into a Learning Community,* edited by Isa Aron, et al., 14–55. New York: UAHC.

Zinn, Lorraine M. 1991. "Identifying Your Philosophical Orientation." In *Adult Learning Methods: A Guide for Effective Instruction,* edited by Michael W. Galbraith, 39–78. Malabar, FL: Krieger.

www.ingramcontent.com/pod-product-compliance
Lightning Source LLC
Chambersburg PA
CBHW071232170426
43191CB00032B/1357

* 9 781498 218764 *